THE FIRST
COMMENTARY
ON MARK

THE FIRST COMMENTARY ON MARK

An Annotated Translation

Translated and Edited by
MICHAEL CAHILL

New York • Oxford

Oxford University Press

1998

Oxford University Press

Oxford New York

Athens Auckland Bangkok Bogota Bombay Buenos Aires
Calcutta Cape Town Dar es Salaam Delhi Florence Hong Kong
Istanbul Karachi Kuala Lumpur Madras Madrid Melbourne
Mexico City Nairobi Paris Singapore Taipei Tokyo Toronto Warsaw

and associated companies in
Berlin Ibadan

Published by Oxford University Press, Inc.
198 Madison Avenue, New York, New York 10016

Oxford is a registered trademark of Oxford University Press

Library of Congress Cataloging-in-Publication Data
The first commentary on Mark : an annotated translation /
translated and edited by Michael Cahill.
p. cm.
Includes bibliographical references and index.
ISBN 0-19-511601-1
1. Bible. N.T. Mark—Commentaries—Early works to 1800.
I. Cahill, Michael. II. Expositio Evangelii secundum Marcum.
BS2585F57 1998   97-1306

1 3 5 7 9 8 6 4 2

Printed in the United States of America
on acid-free paper

For Diane

PREFACE

IT WAS A TURNING POINT in my life when, in 1988, I read Bernhard Bischoff's "Turning-Points in the History of Latin Exegesis in the Early Middle Ages." I was intrigued by what he had to say about a pseudo-Jerome Markan commentary. When I then read this Markan commentary in Migne's PL edition, my first thought was to provide an English translation. My initial attempt made it clear that a critical edition of the Latin text was a necessary first step. Years later, when I had completed this, I determined to provide an annotated English translation of what I had come to recognize as the first Markan commentary. In a sense, then, I am back where I started.

The introductory essay attempts to situate the Markan commentary in its English translation. A full introduction is to be found, properly, in the edition of the Latin text. To this, the reader is referred for a comprehensive and detailed discussion of the issues connected with the text. In the introduction, I have confined my remarks to what needs to be said to facilitate an intelligent reading of the text in English. Some key issues remain unresolved, and I have concentrated on what can be definitely said. The controversial matters can be pursued with the help of the notes and bibliography.

I have learned to live with the frustration of being unable to be more definite in regard to authorship and provenance. I frankly admit to being cautious in the use of conjecture. I see no point in resorting to a process of cumulative hypothesis. It is my hope that the appearance of the text in a new critical edition and in English translation will contribute to eventual certainty in these matters.

I am aware of my debt to the infectious enthusiasm and scholarly support of the circle of Hiberno-Latin scholars who have accompanied me in my exploration of this text over the years. They have been tolerant of my "methodological agnosticism" in regard to provenance! My colleagues in the Department of Theology, Duquesne University, have been constant in their encouragement. Patricia O'Kane of the Gumberg Library at Duquesne University has been unsparing of her expertise. I have benefited from a Duquesne University Presidential Scholarship, which facilitated the completion of this translation; I welcome the opportunity to acknowledge this. My wife, Diane, collaborated in many ways; she has reason to welcome the completion of the project! I have benefited greatly from the advice and guidance of Cynthia A. Read (Executive Editor) and Cynthia L. Garver (Production Editor) of Oxford University Press; I salute their consummate professionalism. I wish to associate myself with the words of the first Markan commentator when he seeks the indulgence of the reader. He acknowledges that he did not perfectly achieve his aims—"ut volui, non valui."

Pittsburgh, Pennsylvania   M.C.
June 1997

CONTENTS

ABBREVIATIONS

I USE AN ABBREVIATED reference system. In the case of the Latin texts, I give samples of the abbreviated reference system used along with the expansions; full details are given in the bibliography. The variations are due to my attempt to facilitate ease of reference to works which are edited and presented in different ways.

Commonly Used Abbreviations

CCCM   *Corpus Christianorum. Continuatio Medievalis.*

CCSL   *Corpus Christianorum. Series Latina* (Brepols).

CPL   *Clavis Patrum Latinorum* (E. Dekkers).

CSEL   *Corpus Scriptorum Ecclesiasticorum Latinorum.*

PG   *Patrologia Graeca* (ed. J. P. Migne).

PIBA   *Proceedings of the Irish Biblical Association.*

PL   *Patrologia Latina* (ed. J. P. Migne).

SC   *Sources Chrétiennes* (Cerf).

Thes. Pal.   *Thesaurus Palaeohibernicus*, I. See Stokes and Strachan.

Latin Texts

Amb *Patr.* p. 133 7. Ambrosius [Ambrose], *De patriarchis* (page and line numbers in CSEL 32).

Amb *Sp* p. 17 47. Ambrosius, *De Spiritu Sancto* (page and line numbers in CSEL 79).

Arnob. Jnr. *Exp* p. 276 94. Arnobius Iunior, *Expositiunculae in Euangelium* (page and line numbers in CCSL 25A).

Aug *Civ* 8:19 p. 326 45–46. Augustinus [Augustine], *De civitate Dei libri 22* (book, chapter, page, and line numbers in CCSL 47–48.

Aug *Conf* xiii, 9. Augustinus, *Confessionum libri 13* (book and section number in CCSL 27).

Aug *Ev* p. 4 25. Augustinus, *De consensu Evangelistarum* (page and line numbers in CSEL 43).

Aug *Iob* p. 157 22–23. Augustinus, *Adnotationes in Iob* (page and line numbers in CSEL 28).

Aug *Ioh* p. 301 1. Augustinus, *In Iohannis Evangelium tractatus 124* (page and line numbers in CCSL 36).

Aug *Pet* p. 153 3–4. Augustinus, *Contra litteras Petiliani* (page and line numbers in CSEL 43).

Aug *Ps* 149 p. 2182 10. Augustinus, *Enarrationes in Psalmos* (psalm, page, and line numbers in CCSL 38–40).

Aug *Quaest* p. 14 94. Augustinus, *De diversis quaestionibus 83 liber* (page and line numbers in CCSL 44A).

Aug *Ser* 54 1269 33. Augustinus, *Sermones* (sermon, column, and line numbers in PL 38).

Aug *Sym* p. 187 58–59. Augustinus, *Sermo de symbolo* (page and line numbers in CCSL 46).

BibW. Anonymous, "Reference Bible" or "Bibelwerk."

Cam 4r 20. Anonymous, "Cambridge Pembroke College Ms. 25" (folio and line numbers in edition of James Cross, q.v.).

C. Arles *Ser* 212 p. 845. Caesarius of Arles, *Sermones* (sermon and page numbers in CCSL 103–104).

Cat. Celt. p. 33 45. Anonymous, *Catechesis Celtica* (page and line numbers in Wilmart, "Catéchèses Celtiques").

Crac 15 p. 15 130. Anonymous, *Catechesis Cracoviensis* (page and line numbers in edition of T. L. Amos, q.v.).

Cyprian *Op* p. 64 292. Cyprian of Carthage, *De opere et eleemosynis* (page and line numbers in CCSL 3A).

Euch *Form* p. 22 7–8. Eucherius, *Formulae* (page and line numbers in CSEL 31).

Euch *Ins* p. 144 1. Eucherius, *Instructionum ad Salonium libri 2* (page and line numbers in CSEL 31).

Euch *Laude* p. 185 16–18. Eucherius, *De laude heremi* (page and line numbers in CSEL 31).

Greg *Cant* p. 40 776. Gregorius Magnus [Gregory the Great], *Expositio in Canticum Canticorum* (page and line numbers in CCSL 144).

Greg *Ez* I 6 pp. 75–77 275–325. Gregorius Magnus, *Homiliae in Hiezechihelem prophetam* (book, homily, page, and line numbers in CCSL 142).

Greg *Hom* 25 1191 C–D. Gregorius Magnus, *Homilia in Evangelia 40* (homily number, column number, and section letter in PL 76).

Greg *Iob* 31 vii p. 1615 50–51. Gregorius Magnus, *Moralium libri sive Expositio in librum Iob* (book, section, and page numbers in CCSL 143B).

Greg *Reg* p. 214 165–167. Grégoire le Grand, *Règle Pastorale* (page and line numbers in SC 381 and 382).

Greg Il *Trac* p. 21 56. Gregorius Iliberritanus, *Tractatus Origenis* (tractate, page, and line numbers in CCSL 69).

Hil *Matt* 9:6, p. 210. Hilaire de Poitiers, *Sur Matthieu* (chapter and verse, page number in SC 254 and 258).

Ioh p. 116 242. Anonymous, "Commentarius in Iohannem" (page and line numbers in CCSL 108C).

Jerome *Dan* p. 863 94–95. Hieronymus [Jerome], *Commentariorum in Danielem libri 3* (page and line numbers in CCSL 143B).

Jerome *Ep* 78 81 22–23. Hieronymus, *Epistulae* (letter, section, and page numbers in CSEL 54–56).

Jerome *Ez* 1 p. 19 459–460. Hieronymus, *Commentariorum in Hiezechielem libri 14* (book number, page, and line numbers in CCSL 75).

Jerome *Hom* pp. 536–537. In Hieronymus, *Tractatus Varii* (page number in CCSL 78).

Jerome *Math* p. 3 55–67. Hieronymus, *Commentariorum in Matheum libri 4* (page and line numbers in CCSL 77).

Jerome *Nom* p. 94 6. Hieronymus, *Liber interpretationis Hebraicorum nominum* (page and line numbers in CCSL 72).

Jerome *Zach* p. 779 60. Hieronymus, *Commentariorum in Zachariam prophetam libri 3* (page and line numbers in CCSL 76A).

Lc p. 12 338–339. Anonymous, "Commentarius in Lucam" (page and line numbers in CCSL 108C).

Mc p. 220 20–24. Anonymous, "Praefacio secundum Marcum" (page and line numbers in CCSL 108B).

Origen *Ex* 12.3 p. 360. Origène, *Homélies sur l'Exode* (homily number with section number and page number in SC 321).

Origen *In Gen Hom* 2 172A. Origenes, *In Genesim* (homily number and column number with letter section in PG 12).

Origen *Jos* 4.1 p. 146. Origène, *Homélies sur Josué* (homily number with section number and page number in SC 71).

Origen *Lev* 3.7 p. 150. Origène, *Homélies sur le Lévitique* (homily with section number and page number in SC 286 and 287).

Origen *Prol* 6 p. 150. Origenes, *Prologus* (section and page numbers in SC 375).

PasR *Math* p. 372 358. Paschasius Radbertus, *Expositio in Matheo* (page and line numbers in CCCM 56, 56A, 56B).

PetC *Ser* 58 p. 326 29–30. Petrus Chrysologus, *Collectio sermonum* (sermon, page, and line numbers in CCSL 24).

PsAl *Sept* 1170 A. Pseudo-Alcuinus, *De septem sigillis* (column number and section letter in PL 101).

PsBed *Coll* 553 B–C. Pseudo-Beda, *Collectanea* (column number and section letter in PL 94).

PsHi *Ev* 512 D. Pseudo-Hieronymus, *Expositio Quatuor Evangeliorum* (column and section letter in PL 30).

PsHil *Iac* p. 54 54. Pseudo-Hilary of Arles, *tractatus in septem epistolas canonicas* (title of epistle, page, and line number in CCSL 108B).

PsIsid *Lib* 1292 D. Pseudo-Isidore, *Liber de ortu et obitu Patrum* (column number and section letter in PL 83).

PsJer *Ev* 533 C. Pseudo-Jerome, *Expositio quattuor Evangeliorum* (column number and section letter in PL 30).

Q Ev p. 150 10–13. Anonymous, "Quaestiones vel glosae in evangelio nomine" (page and line numbers in CCSL 108B).

Rup *Lib*. p. 157 502. Rupertus Tuitiensis, *Liber de divinis officiis* (page and line numbers in CCCM 7).

Sed *Car* I, p. 26 139–140. Sedulius, *Paschale Carmen* (book, page, and line numbers in CSEL 10).

V. Pet *Fab* no. 8. p. 7. Victorinus of Pettau, *De Fabrica Mundi* (section and page number in CSEL 49).

NOTE:

Cf.   When this precedes a reference to a text, it is meant to suggest an allusion, paraphrase, accommodation, or partial correspondence.

THE FIRST
COMMENTARY
ON MARK

INTRODUCTION

The work presented here is the first full-length continuous commentary by a single author on the Gospel according to Mark. In the history of biblical exegesis, it marks an important moment. The work has a significance for the history of biblical exegesis, for the study of patristic exegesis, and for the history of Markan study in particular.

The earliest commentary written on Mark's Gospel has only recently been recognized as such.[1] In his prologue, the Markan commentator observes that Gospel commentators have completely neglected Mark. The fathers of the church left us only homilies on this or that part of Mark, and scholars such as Victor of Antioch fashioned commentaries on Mark which were merely compilations drawn from such patristic efforts. The traditional commentaries on the other three Gospels covered the greater part of the material found in Mark, so that it is understandable that the shortest of the Gospels was neglected. The anonymous author was aware that his was a pioneering effort. Interestingly, he makes explicit mention of the parts proper to Mark, to which, he says, he will give special attention. Ordinarily, the commentator identifies a section or pericope for treatment by briefly quoting the opening and closing phrases and

1. Michael Cahill, "The Identification of the First Markan Commentary." The principal catalogue references to the Markan commentary are the following: Bernhard Bischoff, "Wendepunkte" no. 27; CPL no. 632; Michael Lapidge and Richard Sharpe, *A Bibliography of Celtic-Latin Literature* no. 345. Bibliographical references are given in an abbreviated manner, with full details provided in the bibliography.

then works his way through the pericope commenting as he sees fit.[2] His commentary is by no means exhaustive, and sometimes he omits elements that deserve comment and passes over silently substantial sections of text. But basically it can be characterized as a "running commentary," a line-by-line commentary on the Gospel text, not unlike the kind found today.

Author of the Commentary

Almost a hundred manuscripts are extant of this commentary because during the Middle Ages it was taken to be a work of St. Jerome and widely copied.[3] The Markan commentary received little attention once it was omitted from the canon of the authentic works of St. Jerome by Renaissance scholars. The identity of the author is unknown. Contemporary debate centers on the proposal of Bernhard Bischoff that the author was a seventh-century Irish monk. Certainly, the evidence supports an early-seventh-century date, but Irish authorship needs more positive demonstration.[4] It must be stressed that the recent discussion of the text has been limited to that which has taken place under the auspices of what are termed "Hiberno-Latin Studies."[5] However, given the importance of the work, other possibilities deserve equal consideration. I regard Bischoff's suggestions as to attribution and provenance as "not proven,"

2. It bears mention that the modern reference system of chapter and verse was not available in the early Middle Ages. In order to identify a passage, commentators had to quote parts of the text or mention a specific incident.

3. In my CCSL edition I provide a revision (involving corrections, omissions, and additions) of Bernard Lambert's valuable listing of the manuscripts in his *Bibliotheca Hieronymiana Manuscripta* (no. 473). The most important manuscript for establishing the extent of the original text is "Angers 275," an early-ninth-century manuscript, which, apart from the interpolated homily (see the appendix to this volume), is uniquely free of later additions. Paradoxically, it is the only manuscript to preserve the epilogue.

4. Early in the present century, a brief debate took place about its authorship. It is interesting to note that two experts, Wohlenberg and Morin, differed widely in dating and provenance: late-seventh-century Canterbury and fifth-century Rome, respectively (G. Morin, "Un commentaire romain sur S. Marc"; G. Wohlenberg, "Ein vergessener lateinischer Markuskommentar"). In 1954 the eminent German scholar, Bernhard Bischoff, suggested that the work was authored by the Irish monk Comianus in the first half of the seventh century (Bernhard Bischoff, "Turning-Points," pp. 80–82). Scholars have debated this but without clear outcome (See for example E. Coccia, "La cultura irlandese precarolongia. Miracolo o mito?"; Clare Stancliffe, "Early 'Irish' Exegesis"). Some parallels can be noted in early Hiberno-Latin literature but of a kind that does not speak of an exclusive Irish context and background but rather of the common patristic and literary sources of the Latin West.

5. A helpful survey of this field of scholarship can be found in Martin McNamara's "Celtic Scriptures: Text and Commentaries."

while giving due consideration to the possibility of Irish provenance in the annotations.[6]

There is a clear authorial voice in the commentary. The author refers explicitly to the fact of writing a book, as the opening sentences of both chapters 14 and 16 indicate. He is conscious that he is doing something fresh and new in producing a commentary on Mark. He states his goals at the outset and refers to them from time to time. That he does not always achieve his stated goals is another matter. Twelve times he draws attention to sections of text proper to Mark. In the prologue, he states that he will attend especially to such items, where, incidentally, he numbers them as eighteen. Yet his treatment of these passages is perfunctory, and, apart from the mention of their being proper to Mark, they get no special treatment. A striking feature of the commentary is the enumeration of the fifteen miracles ("virtues") of Jesus.[7] Despite the prominence of this structuring element of his commentary, he does not mention it in his prologue.

He treats the Gospel as a unit and enumerates the sequence of the "acts of power" ("virtues") of Jesus. He frequently harmonizes the Gospel narratives, though at other times he is careful to note the parts that are proper to Mark. A careful reading of the text suggests that he is an abbot of a monastery, writing for cloistered readers. One can discern his voice in the recurrence of favorite topics. He is very interested in the correct understanding and exercise of authority. He has a strong sense of church and of attachment to the church of Rome. His own church is a daughter church of Rome, but it is not clear whether he is referring to his church of origin or church of residence. He is very conscious of his gentile background and of the providential emergence of the church of the gentiles in relation to the continuing existence of the Jews. He appears to be extraordinarily aware of the fact of the Jews, and, while many of his comments are negative, he insists on their ultimate salvation. He has what we would term today a "high Christology" and appears to have written at a time when

---

6. Bischoff's hypothesis as to provenance of the Markan commentary has been prematurely "canonized" by some scholars. For example, the earlier volumes of *Vetus Latina* refer to the author of the Markan commentary as "PS-HI" (Pseudo-Hieronymus); later the reference is to "CU-D" (Cummianus . . . Abt von Durrow" (Bonifatius Fischer, *Verzeichnis der Sigel*, pp. 283–284; cf. E. Dekkers, CPL no. 632; the third edition modifies the position of the earlier editions). In general terms, Michael Gorman calls attention to the limitations of Bischoff's theories about "Irish symptoms." He concludes: "The time has come for the 'main picture' Bischoff presented in 'Wendepunkte' to be examined afresh" ("The Commentary on the Pentateuch Attributed to Bede, pp. 94–96).

7. He omits from his listing the cure of the woman (Mark 5:25) and the walking on the water (Mark 6:48).

teachings of an Arian type about the subordinate nature of Christ were still something to be countered. Unfortunately, such allusions are brief and do not help to situate the work in relation to Arianism in the Latin West, a phenomenon that was widespread in respect to both time and place.

In many cases, medieval biblical commentaries, because of their applied character, are a rich source of information for the historians of church, society, and intellectual life. For example, in recent years, students of Anglo-Saxon have shown great interest in such texts as they attempt to determine sources and spheres of influence in Anglo-Saxon literature.[8] The realities of life are brought into the discussion as practical applications are made. From this point of view, the present commentary is a disappointment because no clear picture of period or place emerges. The sphere of application of the Scriptures is that of the interior spiritual life, the practice of the virtues, and the struggles against the vices. There are occasional allusions to the experience and culture of the author, but unfortunately they are not conclusively clear. Bischoff, for example, argues for Irish provenance from the mention of a boat made of hides stretched upon a wooden frame, which recalls the "currach" still in use in the west of Ireland. Yet such concrete allusions are rare in the Markan commentary, and this lack of application to the normal social-political world lends more support to the view that the cloister was the place where the writing emerged.

Date of the Commentary

Dating the commentary on Mark as seventh century and, more particularly, as belonging to the first half of that century, is to be regarded as reasonable rather then definite.[9] The matter of dating is not helped by the fact that many regard the seventh century as the most obscure in the history of the church. Francis Clark refers to it as "that dark post-Gregorian age."[10] Latinists have not been able to date the work on linguistic grounds. As noted, two of the most authoritative medievalists of this century, Morin and Bischoff, differ widely in their proposed datings. I have established a clear terminus a quo dating by demonstrating the use of the work of Gregory the Great (c. 540–604).[11] This

---

8. The works of James E. Cross and Charles D. Wright are representative (see bibliography).

9. Bischoff proposes that the Markan commentary belongs "most probably to the first half of the seventh century" ("Turning-Points," p. 88). He further notes that it is used in another Gospel commentary (Pseudo-Jerome, "In IV Evangelia"), and this latter he dates c. 700 ("Turning-Points," p. 88–89).

10. Francis Clark, *The Pseudo-Gregorian Dialogues*, vol. 2, p. 745.

11. Michael Cahill, "The Introductory Material," pp. 93–114.

is compatible with Bischoff's suggestion of an early-seventh-century date. I have not been able to identify use by the Markan commentator of any source later than about 600. Another feature of the commentary that is relevant to the dating problem is that the commentator never quotes a nonbiblical source explicitly either in terms of a formal quotation or by naming the authority. Generally speaking, the later the work, the more likely the explicit reference to the Fathers of the Church. We see this, for example, in Bede (c. 673–735). I have not found any sign that the works of Isidore (c. 560–636) were used by the author. In the context of the debate in regard to possible Irish authorship, this corresponds with the scholars' agreement that Isidore's works were not generally known in Ireland before the middle of the seventh century.

Given the lack of clear indicators, we can only analyze the text for possible clues. For example, I have considered possible connections between the commentary's treatment of christological topics and certain controversies and councils. The Lateran Council, held in A.D. 649 (as distinct from the "First Lateran General Council" in A.D. 1123), addressed the issue of the presence of both a human will and a divine will in Christ. Following the urging of Maximus toward the middle of the seventh century, the matter came to a head; the Roman Council insisted that Christ had a human will, which brought the Roman church authorities into direct conflict with Byzantine imperial rule. Such matters would undoubtedly have been well known throughout Europe.[12] On a couple of occasions throughout the course of his commentary, the author gratuitously sees an allegorical pointer to the existence of our free human will but never mentions the will(s) of Christ, as we might expect if he were writing in the latter half of the century. By contrast, his frequent attention to indications of the divinity of Christ fits the earlier half of the century, when variants of the Arian heresy were still the object of lively controversy. This was the legacy of the conflict between the Roman churches and the Visigoths. The Visigoth churches had been converted to an Arian version of Christianity, and unity was achieved only in the late sixth century. However, the variables of Arian influence in regard to place and time make it difficult to use the author's emphasis for a more precise determination of provenance.

A Work of Exposition

In the Latin text, the conjunction *unde* is found a total of 63 times. In deference to the nuances of English usage, I have translated it variously as "there-

---

12. Michael Lapidge provides a helpful treatment of the controversy in his edition of *Biblical Commentaries from the Canterbury School of Theodore and Hadrian* (pp. 70–77).

fore," "thus," "for this reason," "and so." This term is important as it is expressive of the authentic voice of the expositor. I have preferred the Latin title "expositio" for the original Latin text. "Commentary" is the term in use in English today which best describes the genre of the writing, but the Latin term reminds us that it is a work of exposition. The use of the term *unde* helps to specify and characterize the kind of exposition we find in the commentary. The conjunction *unde* in its various English versions is to be taken in its literal conjunctive force as establishing a connection with something else. The commentator aims to show that there is an overall divine plan or logic at work in Mark's story. This can be seen particularly in the case of introducing biblical quotations, which are used to situate Jesus within the overall history of salvation and to demonstrate the coherence of the story with the rest of the biblical text of both testaments. *Unde* is also found when the commentator wishes to extend the application of the story to later generations of Christian disciples. This is presented as an entirely appropriate step in the reading of the Gospel.

Allegory

The commentator's predominant method of reading is allegorical. We must distinguish between a text that is written as an allegory and one that is read allegorically. The commentator understood full well that the Gospel is not an allegory, but he valued the allegorical method of reading for its usefulness. It provided a way of using the sacred text to teach sacred doctrine and allowed the commentator to make applications to the lives of the readers in their pursuit of the virtuous Christian life. Everything is grist for the allegorical mill: characters and their behavior, personal names, animals, numbers, and the physical actions of Jesus. In the prologue, he declares his option for the "mystical" sense. He uses allegory to arrive at this mystical or spiritual sense. This is regarded as superior to the literal sense, though this distinction ignores the fact that frequently the literal sense is itself profoundly mystical or spiritual. There is a conviction operating that the literal sense of the Bible, particularly that of the Old Testament, has to be the vehicle of another superior sense. He reads the text of the Gospel in the service of this other sense. By definition, all allegory has a referent. In this case, we have an allegorical reading of a text that is not in itself an allegory. The commentator reads in reference to, and in the service of, another "text," in this case, a set of teachings which the commentator viewed as the religious syllabus, as lessons to be taught.

In the Markan commentary, we find an emphasis on Christ, on the church, and on the close relationship between them; we find a stress on the practice of the virtues by later generations of disciples in response to the invitation and stimulus of the Gospel text. Teaching on this "syllabus" of topics is deemed important and is presented in an attractive way. In the notes, I draw attention to the commentator's chosen topics as he refers to them. He normally makes only a brief application, and the result is that his treatment is a scattered one. The principal topics merit a more synthetic presentation here. In the footnotes, I draw attention to the significant issues and to the relevant scholarly debate when this has occurred; here I wish to highlight some theological topics of particular prominence.

The Main Theological Interests of the Commentator

The   Church

The commentator uses the term "church" 27 times. This betrays a sense of its importance for him since this term does not occur in Mark's Gospel, the text which is the object of his commentary. The church is the body of Christ; it is the kingdom of God on earth; it is seen as a gentile church, the successor to the Jewish people; it is Roman, with Peter at its head; it is beset by human short-comings; it offers liturgical and sacramental activity through the ministry of bishop and priest; it preaches the gospel to the ends of the earth.

The author is keenly aware of the continuing presence of the Jewish people, and this appears to present a difficulty for him. It would seem that he is not simply responding to the Jews as a literary presence in the pages of the Markan Gospel but that he lives in a society of which Jews were a part.[13] His statements about the Jews are not easy to summarize, as they range from the negative condemnation to the more positive affirmation of the hope of their coming to faith and salvation. In the context of that time, this hope must be classified as positive. There is one memorable positive allusion to the Jews in the commentary on Mark 1:31, where the author refers to Christians as "we, the children of the synagogue" (*nos filii synagogae*). This links the commentator's treatment of the Jews with his ecclesiology.

The Virtuous Life and the Gospel Story

The Christian life to be led by later generations of disciples is seen as the practice of the virtues in response to the example of Jesus, the very first disciples, and other persons and events in the Gospel story. In his prologue, he explicitly

13. As regards this issue, the commentator would be at home in the circumstances of Spain or Southern Gaul. Such speculation, however, needs more positive indications for a fruitful hypothesis to emerge.

refers to the necessity of imitating Jesus in the "examples" to be found in the text. He points out that the series of events presented in quick succession in Mark 1:9–13 is to be seen as providing a moral agenda for us "according to the example of Christ." The stories of other Gospel characters are brought to bear on the lives of later disciples: Peter's uncertainty during the trial (Mark 14:53) is used to draw spiritual lessons; the presence of Mary Magdalene (described as a "widow") and of the other women at the crucifixion (Mark 15:40) reminds us that the feminine gender (*muliebris sexus*) is included in the mysteries of salvation.

This reading of the Gospel text in the terms of ascetical theology is probably the most distinctive feature of the commentary. It is an asceticism practiced in the cloister. The primary audience is certainly a monastic one. This supports the view that the author is an abbot exercising his responsibility of exhorting his monks to Christian perfection. At first sight, this may suggest that the text has a limited value for the nonmonastic Christian disciple. However, the application of the lessons of the Gospel is usually done in strokes broad enough to allow any Christian to recognize their relevance.

Contemporary Interest in the Older Commentaries

There is fresh interest today in the ancient commentaries, due to a combination of causes and circumstances.[14] The historical-critical method has been criticized by some as too coldly scientific and lacking in spiritual nourishment. While maintaining the necessity of the historical method, we can be open to the complementary role of other approaches and methods. It is both challenging and intriguing that there is a great divide between almost 1,900 years of ascendancy of the precritical approach and the last hundred years, when critical research has come into vogue.[15] The precritical era is not, of course, a monolith. Periods can be distinguished, but overall they have much more in common with each other than any of the subperiods has in common with the modern critical period. For much of the greater part of its existence, the church has been fueled by a way of reading the Scriptures that has been largely aban-

---

14. I mention the following as straws in the wind: Seán P. Kealy, C.S.Sp., *Mark's Gospel: A History of Its Interpretation* (1982); Robert Grant with David Tracy, *A Short History of the Interpretation of the Bible*, 2d ed. (the addition of part 2 by Tracy in 1984 to the original work of Grant in 1963 is indicative of the newly emerging interest); Ulrich Luz, *Matthew in History: Interpretation, Influence, and Effects* (1994).

15. I refer here to the time periods in which the respective approaches were reaching the church communities at large in some way, principally through seminary training, and not merely discussed in university circles.

doned today by Bible scholars.[16] The two approaches appear to be so different that they are mutually exclusive. Is there any way to bridge the chasm?

Some of the presuppositions of the ancient biblical commentators may be briefly reviewed as a preparation to a sympathetic reading of the Markan commentary. For them, the whole Bible forms one single unified textual "given." It is seen as an organic whole. Like any organism, the parts affect each other. The meaning of any particular text can be determined and developed by positing a relationship with any other text. They saw the Bible commenting on itself. The basis proposed for each relationship can change, ranging from the simple occurrence of the same word, irrespective of the context, to a similarity of incident or character, even of the most incidental type. Although occasionally the commentator based an allegory or a metaphor on some extrabiblical subject, the principal source is the Bible itself. In this sense, the approach can be said to be essentially a literary one. This tendency to explain one thing in terms of another is a characteristic of the allegorical method. The human mind has an allegory-making ability, but the prevalence of allegory in biblical exegesis is explained, I believe, by attending to the place of esthetics in biblical interpretation.

The Sacred Scripture was seen as having a form or, rather, being composed of forms within forms in a mutually satisfying balance. The "before and after Christ" sequence provided the major but not the only creative tension. Because the one divine author is the ultimate composer, unity and harmony are posited. Because the whole Bible is telling the story of God's salvation of his people, there is a thread running through it all. The parallels and correspondences are there to be discovered by the commentator, to be exposed for the admiration and wonder of the reader. Much of what strikes us as arbitrary and even perverse was, for the medieval mind, very satisfying and totally reasonable. As we see in the case of the present work, this comprehensive view of the Bible is compatible with an awareness of the distinctiveness of each book. In fact, the distinctiveness of each testament and of the diverse components made the search for patterns of similarities and contrast and the discovery of them all the more wonderful to the medieval eye. Having said that, we must still acknowledge that such an approach can entail, at its worst, a frivolous association of ideas without discipline and, at its best, a charming unity, symmetry, and coherence.

---

16. Of course, it has to be acknowledged that the precritical style of reading the Bible, including allegorical reading, never died out in most ecclesial traditions, particularly in the area of piety and devotion, and in homiletic practice.

Patristic commentary was traditional in the sense that each generation saw itself enriched by the contributions of previous ones. Commentary was like a snowball. Previous commentators' work was regarded as an inheritance. It could be taken over, adapted or not, without our modern sensitivity to plagiarism. Later medieval commentary frequently cited explicitly the source used. But in the case of this Markan commentary, we have not yet arrived at this stage.

In such writing, respect for tradition is very strong and leads to the presence of themes and allusions which may be merely conventional rather than indicating the personal experience or circumstances of the writer. When the commentator refers to Arius and other heretics, is he parroting earlier preoccupations or talking about what he personally knows?[17]

Generally, we do not read precritical biblical commentaries to find what we get in the modern critical commentaries.[18] It is to see what sense our ancestors found in the biblical text that we take up the ancient commentaries. It is to see how they applied the text to their lives in a practical way. It is to see what they judged important. The ancient commentaries are to be understood as operating within a pastoral and catechetical context. The basic teaching of the church had been formulated. This teaching was understood as having been derived from the Bible, and the preachers and teachers understood themselves as purveyors of biblical truth. The Bible was then read and commented on in the light of the established "syllabus"; each part of the biblical text was seen as a resource to be used, in turn, to teach each and any biblical teaching.

This Translation

This translation has been done from the new critical edition of the Latin text I prepared for the *Corpus Christianorum* series of Christian Latin texts.[19] This text is different from the version that has been in circulation since the early ninth century and which was published by Migne in the *Patrologia Latina* series.[20] The new CCSL text is purged of later additions. These interpolations can be found in an appendix to the Latin edition, though I have retained one, the

17. In the case of Bede, Lawrence Martin suggests that such references to dead issues are an indication of how Bede respectfully identified with the concerns of his patristic authorities (Bede, *Commentary on the Acts of the Apostles*, p. xxiii).

18. Of course, sometimes the older commentaries contain information of interest to the historicocritical scholar. For example, it is possible to find in the older Latin commentaries important witnesses to biblical text types in that the Latin translation may have been made from Hebrew and Greek manuscripts now lost.

19. *Expositio Evangelii secundum Marcum* (CCSL 82; Turnhout: Brepols, 1997).

20. PL 30:589–644.

most substantial one, in this English translation. It is a homily that is found even in the single manuscript that is free of all the other additions (i.e., Angers 275, an early ninth-century manuscript). Because it has its own interest and charm and has never been translated, I thought it useful to include it as an appendix.

I have attempted to provide a translation in a modern idiom. Latin uses long sentences with subordinate clauses. I have not hesitated to break them down into shorter sentences in English. This means that often I have to supply and repeat the subject of the sentences for clarity's sake. Some constraints arise from the nature of the work. When the commentary demands that the Gospel text be translated and understood in a particular way, at times I have to use a very literal translation to avoid making nonsense of the ensuing commentary. Thus, in the time schedule given for the events of the crucifixion and death of Jesus, I have been unable to transpose the sequence into modern timekeeping. The same applies in the case of weights, measures, and currency.

This commentary is done on the Latin text of the Gospel and uses the Latin text of the Bible.[21] Verbal parallels often depend on the recognition of the use of the Latin text. This Latin translation is different in many details from the versions of the Hebrew and Greek texts taken as authoritative today, so that often the point being made by the commentator is clouded when checked against a modern translation that was made directly from the original biblical languages. This complicates matters for the translator. Generally, and most particularly in the case of the Psalter, the use of modern "equivalency" translations will not be helpful for understanding the ancient Markan commentary. It may help the modern reader to use the Douay-Rheims translation, which was made from the Latin Vulgate, though this translation is scarcely available today.[22]

Presentation of Text

The layout of ancient Bible commentary is different from contemporary practice. This point needs to be attended to, as it influences the content. In the first place, the chapter and verse reference system had not yet been introduced. Modern conventions such as word divisions, punctuation, paragraphs, quota-

21. The text of Mark and of the other biblical books used by the commentator is that of the Vulgate. There are occasional interesting eccentricities that will doubtless contribute to further discussion of provenance with the appearance of the new Latin edition.

22. I give the biblical references in relation to modern translations and enumeration; I follow the reference system of the *New Jerusalem Bible*.

tion marks, and so on are lacking or are different. I have arranged the work to keep as closely as possible to the format of the early medieval manuscripts so that the modern reader can get some idea of how the ancient biblical exegete worked. The resources and conventions of the ancient exegetes affected their manner of commentary, and we appreciate them better if we see their products as accurately as this can be done in English translation.

Different print styles are utilized to facilitate a reading of an ancient text for the modern reader. The section of text commented on is given in bold type. The "lemma," as this portion of text is called, rarely consists of a full verse, and sometimes only a phrase is quoted. Often a pericope is delineated by quoting the opening and closing phrases. I have deliberately retained the older usage and refrained from supplying the full text of the Gospel. The text is presented as it is found in the earliest manuscripts, to the extent of repeating the "etc., as far as" in the biblical passages quoted. I use sporadic bold type to signal some irregularity in the lemmata. Sometimes the commentator quotes an adjusted form of the Gospel text, omitting, adding, or changing words. Occasionally a new section of commentary begins without a lemma.

I have, of course, made some other concessions to the modern reader by supplying chapter and verse references for lemmata and for phrases of, or allusions to, the Markan text occurring in the body of the commentary text. All other biblical references have been confined to footnotes to allow an easier reading line. I have signaled the presence of biblical quotations and allusions by italicizing an entire quotation or key words or phrases. It is good that such a convenient method of signaling the presence of such texts is available to us because it helps to see at a glance that this Gospel commentary is a tissue of biblical quotations, paraphrases, and allusions. It must be remembered that it is notoriously difficult to distinguish clearly between an accurate quotation and a paraphrase or an accommodated form of a text. Sometimes the commentator appears to be quoting from memory; sometimes he combines two similar texts; sometimes he uses a version of the text that represents a variant in terms of modern text criticism. I use sporadic italicization of key words to draw attention to the presence of a biblical text that for some reason cannot be rated as a quotation by the norms of today. Thus, I do not use quotation marks for biblical quotations, except where the beginning of the quotation differs from the biblical text. Normal quotation marks are used for quotations from nonbiblical authors. This procedure also permits the text to be closer to the original, which was unencumbered by references (or indeed by footnotes!).

In respect to the text of the Bible, the Markan commentary is a tissue of quotation, paraphrase, accommodation, and allusion. It will help to check the biblical reference. Frequently, the point made by the commentator will not be understood unless the reference is grasped. In some more difficult cases, I explain or suggest an explanation. Sometimes I admit defeat, in instances where the logic of the commentator puzzles me. In his classic study of monastic learning, Leclercq reminds us that the monastic scholars knew the biblical text so well that one word easily triggered another in what can be termed "concordance exegesis."[23] As suggested earlier, there is an underlying larger and serious purpose operating. Yet at times, it seems that the links between texts are trivial, though the ensuing link may well be used to teach and remind readers of important truths.

In the footnotes, I attempt to provide some minimal guidance for the reader who is unfamiliar with the methods and conventions of biblical commentary of this kind. I try to present enough background information to permit a sympathetic reading. In preparing the notes, I have kept the more general reader in mind along with the scholar. Thus, at times I point out the underlying logic of the commentator's exposition.

References to Sources

While the medieval scholar has recourse to the CCSL edition of the original Latin, I thought it useful to include the principal references to sources and parallels in the Latin editions. The intention here has not been to signal them all, but enough to make clear an essential characteristic of the commentary. The more general reader can simply ignore these references because I explain in the notes the significance of the more important uses of source material. In the case of the more frequently occurring, I give the references to the English translations when available, such as Gregory the Great's homilies on the Gospels.

Reading the Markan Commentary

One of the contemporary trends in biblical studies (and in literary studies in general) emphasizes the role of the reader in the encounter with the text. It is tempting to point to some parallels with the patristic reading of the text. In the contemporary approach, which transcends and even ignores historical and redactional types of methodology, we are curiously close to the patristic approach,

---

23. Jean Leclercq, *The Love of Learning and the Desire for God*, pp. 82–83. This point is developed in regard to Bede by Lawrence T. Martin in his annotated translation of Bede's *Commentary on the Acts of the Apostles* (pp. xxix–xxx).

which placed demands on the ingenuity and creativity of the reader.[24] The most recent and innovative work on Mark involves recognition and analysis of patterns, structures, and inner and outer codes and relationships.[25] The patristic reading of the text of Mark and of the other Gospels is not as far from this as first impressions might suggest. The use of allegory and the close relating of one text with others and with the patterns of human conduct demand a sensitivity to the possibilities of the text and an imaginative ability to see patterns and deeper-than-surface links. Our commentator reads Mark with an eye on the entire biblical narrative and allows the Markan account to awaken echoes and parallels.

Many who have studied the Bible according to the modern critical methods are unprepared for the strange and different world they encounter when they pick up the works of the Fathers. This commentary on Mark is an excellent place to acquire a familiarity with this manner of exegesis, in that it is dealing with a familiar text, Mark, and the commentary is brief. Although coming after the period of the Fathers of the Church, strictly speaking, it is altogether typical of their approach and is, in effect, a compendium of their techniques.

We can view the commentary as a stepping-stone between the patristic era and the Middle Ages. The famous medieval *Glossa Ordinaria* (the General Commentary on the Bible) would draw upon this Markan commentary, as would St. Thomas Aquinas in his *Catena Aurea* (literally "Golden Chain," an anthology of choice passages from the Fathers' biblical commentaries).

Given the date of the commentary, the author is in a position to draw upon the patristic commentary tradition of the East and West insofar as that was known to him. The source analysis I have engaged in shows that the work has a compendious quality in regard to the older authorities. The significance of the weight of the individual sources is difficult to assess. The use of a source such as Jerome's or Eucherius's glossaries could well have been mediated through another source. The use of an idea that ultimately goes back to Origen, for example, does not prove that the author had read Origen. Sometimes an image or idea has become part of the church's anonymous tradition. Ambrose, Augustine, Jerome, and Gregory the Great used the work of the Greek Fathers extensively, and their works, in turn, were quarried by such as the author of the Markan com-

---

24. I develop this point in my article "Reader-Response Criticism and the Allegorizing Reader."

25. The beginning of this phase in Markan studies is charted in the useful review essays by Joanna Dewey ("Recent Studies on Mark") and Vernon K. Robbins ("Text and Context in Recent Studies of the Gospel of Mark").

mentary.[26] Yet, the frequency of parallels with the homilies of both Caesarius of Arles and Gregory the Great suggests that the author was personally familiar with their writings.

The taking over of material can sometimes be slavishly done, especially in technical areas of etymology and philology, but generally the author adapts the source material in a personal way. What we find is a refraction of the patristic source. This results in a commentary that is no mere compilation but a work with its own distinctive voice and structure.

The ancient commentators were attempting to keep the hard core of biblical and revealed teaching close to the people in palatable, easily imaginable, and assimilable form. What has been said will help the reader to situate this commentary within the history of exegesis. Historical perspective facilitates correct expectations of a work. Study of the present commentary shows that the resources of the entire Bible, stories, ideas, language, and imagery are put at the service of a select number of points of doctrine, which are regarded as central to Christian faith and which have their origin in the Bible itself. What is noteworthy is that this commentary represents the first time that the Gospel according to Mark was deliberately read as a whole and pressed into the service of the religious enterprise.

26. Denis Brearley writes: "A preliminary comparison of the Angers BM 275, Vienna 997, and PsJerome (PL 30) [the present commentary on Mark] commentaries suggests that all three may have drawn upon earlier (and as yet still unidentified) collectanea or collections of patristic and late-patristic excerpts, along with Biblical glosses" ("The 'Expositio Iohannis' in Angers BM 275," p. 157, n. 43).

PROLOGUE

Every scribe who has been instructed in the kingdom of heaven is like a householder who can show off old and new items from his collection of precious things.[1] However, I am like the poor widow tossing her *two mites* into the treasury.[2] I do this for my poor students who expect to get nourishment from a lean satchel. I am contributing those little crumbs that fall from the table of rich people. My puppies clamor for them as eagerly as the Tyro-Phoenician woman did, anxious for her daughter.[3] I have nothing at all like *gold, silver and jewels*,[4] but I do offer, if I can, *vellum pages—hyacinth* ones dealing with heavenly realities, and *red* ones about earthly matters.[5] I will, with God's help, exert myself to make known

1. Matt 13:52. In early medieval biblical commentary, the prologue was designed to provide useful information to the reader of the Gospel concerning authorship and design of the work. Much of what follows here, particularly in the second half, is not linked specifically with the Gospel of Mark. The purpose of Gospel reading is said to be the imitation of Christ and the stirring up of the basic virtues, especially reverential fear, faith, hope, and charity, of which the Gospel material is full. The writer draws attention to the sections proper to Mark. Another feature of his commentary is the way he enumerates and comments on the 15 miracles ("virtutes") performed by Christ in Mark's account. Yet he does not refer to this in his prologue. This makes it likely that he is taking over material from another source.

2. Cf. Mark 12:41–42; Luke 21:2.

3. Cf. Mark 7:24–30 and parallels (par.). The peculiar form "Tyrophoenician" has been retained instead of the usual "Syrophoenician" because it is also found in Adomnan's *De Locis Sanctis* (p. 221 12) and so may prove to be helpful in determining provenance.

4. 1 Cor 3:12; cf. Acts 3:6.

5. The fact that the same material (skins) is used for the tabernacle and for writing the present commentary allows the expositor scope for an imaginative development. Cf. Ex

the story, or rather the mystical sense, of Mark the Evangelist, which my predecessors have handed on to me.[6]

It seems to me that the reason Gospel commentators have completely neglected him is because he tells much the same story as does Matthew.[7] However, they are different in the declarations proper to each. It is like the way the
wings overlap each other in the case of the *animals*, or just as one *wheel* goes in
the same direction as the other; Mark and Matthew are like the sacred *animals*
who turn their *faces* to gaze at each other.[8]

In the first table Mark can be lined up with Matthew and Luke, together
with John.[9] In the second table he can be compared with Matthew and Luke;

25:5; 26:14; 35:7, 23; 36:19; 39:33. Gregory the Great in his *Pastoral Care* (p. 50) associates
the color with the sky, representing the love of heavenly things. This can be traced back to
earlier authorities. Cf. Jerome, *Ez* 1 p. 19 459–460; PsHil *Iac* p. 54 54. It is possible that the
color red represents martyrdom experienced on this earth.

6. Greg *Hom* 33 1242 A. Technical terms are used here. *Historia* (story) can also be translated as "literal sense." The author points out that he wishes to concentrate on the spiritual
or mystical sense. There is a genuine difficulty of terminology here. "Literal" cannot always be opposed to "spiritual" since often, for example, the literal sense is the spiritual
sense. "Predecessors" translates the Latin *majores*, which literally means "betters." The author acknowledges his dependence on earlier commentators. Commentators of this period
did not see themselves apart from the exegetical tradition.

7. The writer is conscious that he is the first.

8. Cf. Ps 16:8; cf. Ezek 1 passim; Ex 25:20. Jerome *Math* p. 3 55–67; Greg *Ez* I 6
pp. 75–77 275–325; Greg *Hom* 25 1191 C–D; PsHi *Ev* 533 C; Euch *Form* p. 22 7–8, p. 43
14–16. The author is drawing on traditional imagery here. His immediate source is a homily on Ezekiel 1 by Gregory the Great, which the author presents in a telescoped and con-
fusing manner. The winged cherubim are taken to represent the four evangelists. In a way
typical of patristic exegesis, Gregory switches imperceptibly to another set of cherubim in
Ex 25, where the two cherubim face each other over the ark of the covenant. Gregory
points to the OT and NT. Here the image is altered to evoke the well-known image of
the fourfold witness of the evangelists to Christ. The winged cherubim in Ezek 1 with four
different faces have been associated with the four evangelists from the time of Irenaeus.
The link is found in Jerome and Augustine, although Augustine's distribution is different.
The image of the wheel within a wheel is linked with the animals in Ezek 1 and 10. Gregory's
fuller and more expanded treatment of the imagery in his homily on this text makes a clearer
transition between the sets of cherubim and indicates that the commentator is summariz-
ing it (cf. Gregory, *Forty Gospel Homilies*, p. 191). This helps to establish the direction of
the influence and determines the dating of the Markan commentary as post-Gregory.
Gregory's understanding of the two cherubim of Exodus 25 in relation to the two testaments is found also in Eucherius, where it is linked with the text of Habakkuk 3:2 in the
Old Latin version: "In medio duorum animalium innotesceris" (*Form* p. 43 14–16; cf. p. 22
7–8). Such usage all goes to make up the rich store of imagery that was available in the
tradition of biblical commentary.

9. Cf. Wordsworth and White, *Novum Testamentum*, pp. 7–10; Weber et al., *Biblia Sacra*,
2:1516–1526. The calculations here depend on what are sometimes called the "Ammonian
Sections" but more commonly the "Eusebian Canons," after Eusebius of Caesarea (c. 260–c.
340). This is a system of identifying the sections of the Gospel text with a particular interest

in the fourth, with Matthew and John; in the sixth, like two rings on a pole,
Matthew is always linked with Mark, that is in 48 sections.[10] In the eighth table,
Mark is accompanied by Luke, namely in 13 sections. I intend to concentrate
on explaining what is found only in Mark, which is contained in 18 sections.[11]
Altogether, there is a total of 233 sections.[12]

"Mark, the Evangelist of God, the disciple of Peter, a Levite by birth and a
priest, wrote this gospel in Italy."[13] He took the "opening" of his Gospel "from
the words of the Prophets." He uses the testimony of Malachi, that is, messen-
ger, to support John the forerunner of Christ.[14] He points to "the Word made
flesh" in the words of Isaiah. He established the source of "the preaching of
the good news." What he had lost in written letters by leaving out the gene-

---

in noting the correspondences between the Gospels, somewhat like modern Gospel parallels or synopses. There are some slight variations of numbers in the manuscripts. Some of
the numbers are again recorded at the end of the commentary. Other, probably Irish, writings
on the Gospels have variations: Matthew and Mark with 47 in common, Mark with a total
of 232, and 18 sections proper to Mark (*Mc* p. 221 33–35).

Maura Walsh and Dáibhí Ó Cróihín, in a recent survey of the issue of possible Irish
authorship, comment: "Against these suggested indications of Irish/Insular origin, however, must be set the facts that . . . the passages peculiar to Mark's Gospel are reckoned to
be 18 in number, whereas they are normally said to be number 19 (as, e.g., in the book of
Durrow" (*Cummian's Letter*, p. 221).

10. Cf. Ex 25:13–14. The Gospels were imaged as the rings on the four corners of the
ark, which was carried on two poles. This imagery is found in Gregory the Great, *Pastoral
Care*, p. 87.

11. The commentator explicitly mentions whenever a particular section is found only
in Mark, but he can scarcely be said to carry out his intention of concentrating on these
passages.

12. The text of Mark is divided into 233 sections in the Eusebian canons.

13. Traditional Gospel prologue material is used here; I indicate it by quotation marks.
Most ancient copies of the Gospel were prefaced by what came to be known as the Anti-
Marcionite and the Monarchian prologues. The author draws upon the ancient material
while avoiding the obscure and even heretical elements (Cf. Dom John Chapman, *Notes
on the Early History of the Vulgate Gospels*, chapter 15, "The History of the Prologues,"
p. 272ff). Jürgen Regul's more recent study distinguishes two separate texts, the "Anti-
Marcionite Prologues" and the "Monarchian Prologues." These were subsequently combined in the tradition, and elements of both are found in the present prologue (see Regul,
Die Antimarcionitischen Evangelienprologe, esp. pp. 29–30, 47–48). I present a more detailed
examination of the material in my article "The Introductory Material." These prologues
have always been difficult to understand but were highly regarded because of their traditional quality. Our commentator adds his own clarifications, such as his remarks about the
omission of the genealogies found in Matthew and Luke. Each item has been questioned
by modern scholars in regard to its historical value, but this was standard information in
the early medieval world. Mark is said to be cousin of Barnabas (Col 4:10), and Barnabas is
said to be a Levite (Acts 4:36).

14. The mention of Malachi as the source of part of the OT quotation attributed to
Isaiah in Mark 1:2–3 is normal in the early commentaries.

alogies of God and man, "he recovered in the spoken word." He begins to preach from the time of Christ's maturity, "all at once." He writes of the Son of God as fully developed; he does not expend energy on the birth of an infant. He compresses "a whole lot in his brief account" of the "fast of required duration," of the repulse of "the devil, and of the care given by the angels."[15]

Mark was "the first bishop of Alexandria. He had to know in detail the sayings of the Gospel in themselves and then arrange them. He had to acknowledge the discipline of the Law on its own terms.[16] He had to understand the divine nature in the flesh of the Lord."

He sows after Matthew. He roars like a lion. He soars like an eagle. He teaches like a human being.[17] He offers sacrifices just like a priest. He irrigates like a river. He blossoms like Spring. He inflames like wine does. The Christ he speaks of is indeed "a man in his birth, a calf in his death, a lion in his resurrection, and an eagle in his ascension."[18]

The holy Gospels comprise materials of four kinds: precepts, commandments, testimonies, and examples.[19] Justice is established through the precepts, love through the commandments, faith through the testimonies, and perfection through the examples. Precepts—as when Jesus ordered his twelve disciples: *You are not to go into the way of the gentiles.*[20] This means to turn away from evil. Commandments—when he says, *I am giving you a new commandment, that you*

---

15. *Mc* p. 220 20–24.

16. *Disciplina* can also mean "teaching."

17. I translated *discit* as "teaches"; this late Latin usage seems to make better sense than "learns."

18. PsHi *Ev* 534 A; Greg *Iob* 31 p. 1615 50–51; Greg *Ez* I 4 p. 47 29–31; p. 48 36–37; *BibW* as quoted by McNally "The Evangelists," p. 120; PsBed *Coll* 551 C. This paragraph contains a triple series of images that in other writings were applied differently. Eucherius has the sequence: Matthew—human being; Mark—lion; Luke—ox; John—eagle (*Ins* pp. 105–106), but he also has the lion as the symbol for Christ (*Form* p. 25). The series "sows—inflames" is found in other writings but distributed among the four evangelists. In other early writings, there are similar examples of Matthew ploughing, Mark sowing, Luke irrigating, and John supplying wine. See R. McNally, "The Evangelists in the Hiberno-Latin Tradition," for a convenient survey of the source material. In the third series, the images of the evangelists are transferred to Christ; this is a quotation of Gregory the Great (*Iob* 31 p. 1615 50–51). The distribution of the four images is found with some variations in the tradition. The sequence found here is not that of Ezek 1, which is that of the modern sequence of the four Gospels.

19. Q *Ev* p. 150 10–13. There is a touch of the Greco-Roman classical education to be noted here. In rhetoric, literary analysis was taught, and this involved categorization of the contents of a work. The application of the biblical texts strikes us today as contrived and forced. *Exempla* could also be translated as "illustrations" or "anecdotes."

20. Matt 10:5.

should love one another,[21] that is to say, do good and fulfil love. Testimonies—
These are found *in the mouths of two or three witnesses,*[22] as in this one: *John gave
testimony to me but I have a testimony greater than that of John. The Father himself,
who dwells in me, gives testimony to me. And the very works that I perform testify to
me, and I give testimony to the truth.*[23] Examples call for the imitation of Jesus as
when he says, *Learn from me that I am meek,* etc., and *Be perfect, that is compassionate, just as your heavenly Father is perfect.*[24] Elsewhere he says, *I have given you
an example so that you will do likewise.*[25]

Let the verses of the Psalmist sing of these four kinds of material, saying:
The clear precept of the Lord gives light to the eyes.[26] Precepts contain the literal
sense above all.[27] We read in another place, *Your commandment is exceedingly
broad.*[28] This is because *whoever loves their neighbor has fulfilled the whole law.*[29]
Next, *I have understood your testimonies.*[30] For in fact not everyone can understand testimonies. For this reason, he says elsewhere, *The testimony of the Lord is
trustworthy,*[31] because a testimony calls for the faith of the soul more than for
the eyes of the flesh. Fourthly we read, God's *judgments are true, justified in themselves.*[32] That is, let the examples of our judgments be justified like this, as we
ascertain them in God's judgments. In another place, the same seer says, *For I
revere your judgments.*[33] We will be judged *by the same standard* that we have used
to judge.[34]

Reverential fear, faith, hope and love are found in these four kinds of material.[35] For we begin in fear, in faith we persevere in what we have begun, we

21. John 13:34.
22. Cf. Matt 18:16 (Deut 19:15).
23. John 5:36 with intrusions from John 14:10 and 18:37.
24. Matt 11:29; Matt 5:48 with Luke 6:36.
25. Cf. John 13:15.
26. Ps 19:8.
27. Gregory teaches that moral teaching is derived from the literal meaning. Gregory
the Great, *Forty Gospel Homilies*, p. 371.
28. Ps 119:96.
29. Cf. Rom 13:8.
30. Ps 119:95.
31. Ps 19:7.
32. Ps 19:9. The four topics drawn from the work of the Psalmist are not exactly parallel with the four topics previously listed. The four terms are found almost as synonyms in
Pss 19 and 119, for example. The author has clearly compiled elements from various sources
and was prepared to stretch meanings to get the required accommodation.
33. Ps 119:120.
34. Cf. Matt 7:2.
35. The use of a foursome resulting from the addition of fear to faith, hope, and charity is typical of the ingenuity that commentators of this type used to produce work with a
strong catechetical content and pattern.

are encouraged through hope and we achieve perfection in love, for *love is the purpose of precept.*[36] These are the same *four months* which Christ foretold before the harvest, when he said, *Are there not four months until the harvest?*[37]

May we also, after the judgment, joyfully gather ripe fruit, as a result of the precepts, commandments, testimonies and examples of God. Let us reap joyfully in heaven, those seeds of penance that we with fearful *tears* sowed on earth—there *we will carry our sheaves* of love.[38]

END OF PROLOGUE

36. Cf. 1 Tim 1:5. Previously, these four categories are linked with justice, love, faith, and perfection. Such inconsistency suggests that the author of the prologue is compiling from different sources, or perhaps that his original work was added to by a later writer.

37. John 4:35. This interpretation differs from that found in another short commentary identified as Irish, where we read "Four months, that is to say four laws" (*Ioh*, p. 116 53).

38. Cf. Ps 126:5–6.

C H A P T E R   I

The beginning of the Gospel of Jesus Christ, the son of God, etc., as far as **his paths** (Mark 1:1–3).

Εὐαγγέλιον it says in the Greek and it means "good news" in English.[1] It particularly refers to the kingdom of God and to the remission of sins. For that reason it is said, *Repent and believe the gospel* (Mark 1:15b), and *the kingdom of heaven has come.*[2]

Jesus Christ, that is "anointed savior"; in Hebrew "Jesus Messias," It is σωτὴρ χριστὸς in Greek and "anointed savior" in English.[3] This means that he is both king and priest, since Christ is born of the line of David the King, and, in the words of the prophets, he is foretold to be of Levitical descent.[4]

---

1. The original text gives the meaning in Latin ("Latine").
2. Matt 4:17. The use of the version of Matthew is to be noted. Mark 1:15 reads "the kingdom of God."
3. The original Latin text reads *in Latino salvator unctus*. The manuscripts contain corrupt echoes of words and phrases in Greek. The author probably knew enough Greek to copy such from sources but copyists did not.
4. *Q Ev* p. 147 483–484; Aug *Ev* p. 4 25–p. 5 1; p. 6 3–4; Aug *Ps* 149 p. 2182 10; Aug *Quaest* p. 124 94; Amb *Patr* p. 133 7. The Hebrew and Greek etymologies of the venerated name of Jesus Christ were standard material in the commentary tradition. The dual descent of Christ along kingly (Davidic) and priestly (Levitical) lines was part of the traditional reading of Matthew and Luke (see Euch *Ins* p. 106 21–22; p. 107 7–8).

Thus, it continues, **As it is written in the prophet Isaiah, "A voice of one crying in the desert, 'Prepare the way of the Lord,'"** etc. (Mark 1:2–3).[5]

The voice is John. The Lord Jesus referred to this voice when he cried out to the Jews that *among those born of women*, none was greater than he.[6] However, a cry is usually needed for deaf people, or for those a long way off, or it arises out of indignation. These three certainly happened in the case of the Jewish people: since salvation is a long way off from sinners; they *closed* their *ears* and they were as *deaf adders;*[7] they deserved to hear indignation, anger and rebuke from Christ.[8]

A voice, indeed a shout, was heard in the desert. This was because they were deserted by the Spirit of God, exactly like the house that been cleared and swept out.[9] They were deserted by prophet, king and priest.[10] For this reason, John and Jesus seek what was lost *in the desert.*[11] There, where the devil was victorious, now he is defeated. Where man fell, there he arises.[12]

Behold, I send my angel (Mark 1:2).

The voice of πνεύματος ἁγίου [of the Holy Spirit], through Malachi, addresses the Father concerning the υἱῶ [Son] who is the face of the Father, from which he is known.[13] Ἄγγελος [Angel], indeed, means an "announcer," refer-

---

5. The text is compressed.

6. Cf. Matt 11:11 par.

7. Cf. Ps 58:4.

8. Generalized criticism of the Jews of John's and Jesus' time become standard among Christian theologians and Bible commentators. It had a basis in some New Testament texts whose authors spoke in general terms about the rejection of Christ. As we will see, the commentator's attitude to Jews is not entirely condemnatory.

9. Cf. Matt 12:44.

10. Cf. Jer 2:26.

11. Cf. Luke 15:4; 19:10.

12. This may be an allusion to the sins of the Israelites in the desert (Ex 32), but I am inclined to think it is a mistaken adaptation of a contrast between "paradise" and "desert" found in an eulogy of desert hermits by Eucherius. Eucherius writes: *O laus magna deserti, ut diabolus qui vicerat in paradiso in heremo vinceretur* ("What a wonderful place the desert is! The devil who conquered in paradise, is overcome in the desert") (Euch *Laude* p. 185 16–18).

13. *Lc* p. 12 338–339; C. Arles *Ser* 212 p. 845. The trinitarian interpretation is normal in this kind of exegesis. Any text with a triad is liable to be treated like this. Here, the speaker in Mal 3:1 is identified as the Holy Spirit speaking to Father concerning the announcer, Christ. In the very next line, the commentator comfortably shifts back to the literal sense, in which the announcer is John the Baptist. The doctrine of the Holy Trinity is in place and will be expressed in any convenient vehicle. The doctrine is not extracted from this Bible text. Comment on the text provides an occasion for a statement about it.

ring to John who pre-announced concerning Christ: *After me comes someone who was made before me because he was before me.*[14]

He will prepare your way (Mark 1:2).

The way of the Lord, by which he comes to us, is repentance. It is by repentance that God descends to us and we ascend to him. The angels *ascending and descending* bring to mind *the Son of Man.*[15]

Prepare the way of the Lord (Mark 1:3).

That is, "repent and preach." In the same way, the day before the sabbath is called "Preparation Day."[16] This points to the repentance which precedes future rest. The preaching of John and of Jesus has its origin here: *Repent, the kingdom of heaven has drawn near.*[17] Because the Lord *rested* from all his labors *on the seventh day.*[18] We need to destroy by repentance the seven vices as if they were the wicked nations of Canaan, so that afterwards we can rest in possession of *the desirable land.*[19]

Make straight his paths (Mark 1:3).

We have twisted these paths by veering off to right and left.[20] Now we are ordered to enter upon the royal road,[21] and to love our neighbors as ourselves, and ourselves as our neighbors.[22] For whoever loves iniquity *hates his own soul.*[23] Whoever loves himself and not his neighbor veers off to the right. But if he

14. John 1:30.
15. Cf. John 1:51.
16. This explanation was available in Eucherius (*Form* p. 58 8).
17. Matt 4:17.
18. Cf. Heb 4:4.
19. Cf. Deut 7:1; Jer 3:19 (= Ps 106:24); Zech 7:14; Mal 3:12. The number 7 triggers off an association with the seven vices, imaged as the seven nations of Canaan who were to be eradicated according to Deut 7:1. The Old Irish gloss on the Markan commentary specifies the number of the nations as seven ("Turin Glosses," in *Thes. Pal.*, p. 486, line 10). Eucherius relates the nations of Deut 7:1 to the seven vices (*Form*, p. 58 8). This free association of text is altogether typical of patristic (and rabbinical) exegesis, and, while it results in some extraordinary links, there is some control arising from the point that the commentator has to make. The *Catechesis Celtica* lists eight vices (p. 51, l. 165); Maura Walsh and Dáibhí Ó Cróinín notes that Gregory has eight (*Cummian's Letter*, p. 219). In relation to the *Penitential of Cummean*, Bieler notes that "the penances are grouped according to the eight capital sins as formulated by Cassian" (*The Irish Penitentials*, p. 5). Note how we conclude with "homeland," which recalls the "eternal rest" at the beginning of the paragraph.
20. Cf. Num 20:17; cf. Is 30:21.
21. Cf. Num 20:17; 21:22; James 2:8.
22. Cf. Mark 12:31 par.
23. Cf. Prov 29:24.

hates himself and loves his neighbor, he veers off to the left. Many behave correctly but do not correct others well. Such a one was Eli.[24] Many are good at correcting others but do not perform well themselves. Such were the scribes and pharisees who *sat in the chair of Moses.*[25] For this reason, the law requires that the beak of the turtledove be twisted back to its pinions.[26] Let not the pair be broken up.[27] So let not our actions differ from what we say.

The *paths* follow after the *way* because the moral precepts are listed after repentance. They are smoothened, according to Mark.[28] The *way* is prepared though faith, baptism and penance. The *paths* are made straight by proofs of austerity, such as the hair shirt, the leather loincloth, locusts for food, wild honey for drink, and a most humble voice.[29]

And so it follows: **John was in the desert,** etc. (Mark 1:4).

"John" means the "grace of God."[30] The story begins with grace.

For this reason, it continues: **baptizing** (Mark 1:4).

Grace is given through baptism, by means of which sins are graciously forgiven. It is said, *What you have freely received, freely give.*[31] And the Apostle says,

---

24. Cf. 1 Sam 2:12–17; Greg *Reg* p. 214 165–167. Eli failed to correct his two sons, described as scoundrels. Gregory uses the same example more than once (Gregory the Great, *Pastoral Care*, pp. 65–66).

25. Cf. Matt 23:2–4.

26. Lev 1:15–17; 5:8b.

27. Jerome *Nom* p. 94 6; p. 119 19; p. 142 27. Here the writer makes a clever pun derived from Latin grammar that is impossible to translate literally. He wants to graphically express the idea that two elements belong together and should not be separated. I use an equivalent English expression.

28. Cf. Is 40:4. A similar point is made by Gregory (*Forty Gospel Homilies*, p. 8). Given the author's stated intention, the phrase "according to Mark" is noteworthy but puzzling, since there is nothing distinctively Markan in the use of the Isaian text. Only Mark quotes the Malachi text in this context, and only Mark has John's preaching of penance immediately after the "way/paths" text. Yet the motif of "smoothening" (*explanantur*) is an echo only of the source text of Isaiah 40:4 (*in vias planas*). These considerations do not seem to support the author's claim. The marks of John's austere life are equally found in Matthew.

29. Cf. Mark 1:6.

30. Jerome *Nom* p. 146 16–17; p. 155 19; Euch *Ins* p. 144 1. The etymology of names is important in the Bible itself and in the early commentary tradition. Almost always the traditional etymology is followed, as found in either Eucherius and Jerome. The authoritative source in the Latin West was Jerome's "Glossary of Hebrew Names" (*Liber Interpretationis Hebraicorum Nominum*). Jerome prepared his work in consultation with Jewish scholars. There is a certain amount of fanciful or folk etymology in the explanations proposed. This use of etymology is to be classified under the allegorical sense. The ancients were prepared to see a mystical significance in names.

31. Cf. Matt 10:8.

By grace you are saved, through faith, and not of yourselves. The gift is God's
... lest anyone boast.[32]

And preaching a baptism of penance for the remission of sins (Mark 1:4).

What the bridegroom finishes is started by the best man.[33] It is the same for
the catechumens, that is, those who are instructed. They begin with the priest
and are anointed with chrism by the bishop.[34] Now however, the bride is led
in by the friend of the bridegroom, just as in the biblical passage, Rebecca,
with her head covered in a veil, was said to be led by the servant of Isaac.[35]

And the whole region of Judea and all the people of Jerusalem were going out to him and were baptized by him in the River Jordan, confessing their sins (Mark 1:5).

Confession and beauty in his sight,[36] that is, in the sight of the bridegroom.
Just as the bride humbled herself by sliding down from her camel,[37] so does
the Church, now that she sees the true Isaac, Jesus Christ.[38] God made Sarah
laugh at Isaac's birth,[39] while Mary, who is a "princess" in God's sight,[40] is
addressed in the words, *Blessed are you among women.*[41]

"Jordan" means "foreign descent,"[42] where sins are washed away. The
wandering Ark, having forded the Jordan, crossed into an alien land through

---

32. Cf. Eph 2:8–9.

33. The imagery is imported from John 3:29–30. Such a tendency to harmonize the
Gospel accounts was normal.

34. The commentator refers to the liturgical rites and customs of his time. They reflect
those of the Latin West.

35. Cf. Gen 24:65.

36. Ps 96:6a. Euch *Ins* p. 144 13–14. My translation attempts to convey the word link
of the Latin, *confitentes/confessio*, which seems to have evoked the quotation.

37. Cf. Gen 24:64.

38. The patriarchs, together with other characters in the OT, were seen as types of
Christ. Ingenious and fanciful parallels were traced between details of their stories and the
life and character of Christ. Cf. Gen 21:6.

39. Cf. Gen 21:6.

40. Euch *Ins* p. 141 4; Jerome *Nom* p. 150 25; p. 151 7; p. 153 1; p. 157 14. The writer
takes the traditional sense of the name Sarah and applies it to Mary. The Old Irish Gloss
takes it as the meaning of "Mary" (*Thes. Pal.* p. 488, ll.25–26). My translation, "princess,"
attempts to retain the force of the Latin *princeps*.

41. Luke 1:28.

42. Jerome *Nom* p. 67 20; p. 140 27; *Ep* 78 81 22–23; *Nom* p. 85 13; Origen *Prol* no. 6
150. The etymology is problematic. Jerome explains "Jordan" as simply "their descent"
while he explains "Zarath" (Num 21:12) as "alien or descent." The similarity suggests the
possibility of confusion on the part of the author when he was consulting the glossary. Origen

the waters.[43] Half of the river flowed on down to the sea, and the other part piled up, swollen like a mountain.[44] In the same way, we were once alienated from God through pride.[45] By the Creed of baptism we are humbled and then lifted up on high.[46] For *whoever humbles himself will be exalted.*[47] On the other hand, the part that flows into the sea is made bitter.[48] The ark of God, that is the body of Christ, with the commandments, was of no benefit to this part.[49] Indeed, it made it worse.

It continues: **And John was dressed in camelskins,** etc. (Mark 1:6).

The clothes of prophecy, the food, and the drink signify the entire austere life of preachers. They also signify the nations who in the future were to be joined, near and far, to "the grace of God," which is John. The *camelskins* surely stand for the rich ones of the nations;[50] the *leather loincloth,* the poor who are dead to the world; the sharp-edged *locusts,* the wise of this world who leave the dry stubble to the Jews, and who extract mystical grain from the ears, and

---

explains "Zered" in a identical manner that is puzzling in itself. In the prologue to his commentary on the Song of Songs, he gives "a foreign descent" as the meaning of the "Valley of Zered" (*The Song of Songs*, p. 48). The connection with the present text is not clear.

43. Cf. Josh 3:14–16. The ms variants here suggest that the author's meaning was never clear. I have considered the possible influence of Sedulius's *Carmen Paschale* here. The crossing of the Red Sea is understood as a type of baptism by Sedulius, just as the crossing of the Jordan is presented here by the commentator. The poem reads: *perque profundum / Sicca peregrinas stupuerunt marmora plantas* (literally: "And through the deep, the dry sea astonished the foreign soles") [*Carmen Paschale* I, p. 26 139–140; l.143 treats of baptism). *Marmora* presents a difficulty; it means "marble" but it is also used poetically for the sea.

44. Cf. Josh 3:13–16.

45. The fact that the Ark was in foreign parts before arriving "home" is a symbol of our being distant from God.

46. C. Arles *Ser* 97 p. 397 no. 381; 115 p. 478 no. 457 (Latin: *per baptismi symbolum*). It is tempting to translate as "symbol" or "sacrament," but the term appears to be used for "creed" at this time. The Old Irish Turin gloss explains *symbolum* as the creed recited at baptism (*Thes. Pal.*, p. 488, l. 12). There is probably an allusion to the primitive rite of immersion: the crossing of the Jordan is seen as foreshadowing of baptism. There is more than one example in Origen e.g.: . . . *tibi, Christiane, qui per baptismi sacramentum Iordanis fluenta digressus* (Origen, *Jos* 4.1 p. 146); in translation: . . . for you, Christian, who through the sacrament of baptism, parted the waters of the Jordan." Some of Origen's work was known in the West in Latin translation. In Greek (the language of Origen), the parallel Joshua/Jesus was facilitated. This whole passage recalls Origen on Joshua, but it is not a slavish copy.

47. Cf. Matt 23:12.

48. The nature of the Dead Sea or Salt Sea is correctly noted. Later (at Mark 4:1), the Sea of Galilee is also thought to be salty.

49. Euch *Form* p. 51 19.

50. Cf. Is 60:6.

who in the heat of faith make leaps.[51] The *wild honey* represents the inspired faithful emerging from the wild wood, which was prepared for the fires.[52] All of these are taken up by the grace of the Gospel, in which there is no *distinction between Jew and Greek.*[53]

And he was preaching: "After me there comes one more powerful than I" (Mark 1:7).

Who is more powerful than the grace by which sins are washed away? Surely the one who forgives sins *seven* and *seventy* times.[54] Grace indeed comes first but forgives only once through baptism. Now, mercy has arrived for wretches from Adam to Christ for 77 generations, even up to 144,000.[55]

I am not worthy to loose, etc. (Mark 1:7).

"Grace" alone is not worthy *to stoop down* in baptism *to loose the strap of his sandals,* that is, the mystery of the incarnation of God.[56] The heel is the lowest

---

51. Greg *Iob* 31 pp. 1582–1583 15–18.

52. Euch *Form* p. 17 18; Greg *Hom* 36 1270 D. There are many variants in the manuscript transmission of this passage. My translation attempts to make literal sense, but the precise meaning is not clear. The motifs occur in the tradition in a variety of ways.

53. Rom 10:12. The passage is a sustained allegory. The Old Irish Gloss sees a reference to both Jews and gentiles in the phrase "at home and abroad." The camels are associated with the nations because of Is 60:6, which was well known on account of its use at Epiphany. Leather, the skin of dead animals, is a favorite image of the writer. The contrast between stubble and grain will be applied in the area of scriptural interpretation later. Apart from the mention of fires, a similar use of the imagery of locusts and honey is found in Gregory's commentary on Job, as noted previously. He lists the various possible meanings that locusts may have: the converted gentiles and the life of preachers, just to mention the ones that arise in the present text. The leap of the locusts is like the life of the preacher, engaged in the active apostolate, who occasionally aspires to heavenly contemplation but must return to earth. This is close to the thought of the commentator. The honey represents the sweetness that the Redeemer can find among the gentiles. The gentiles are commonly seen as associated with woods. For example, Gregory understands the "trees of the wood" in Ps 96:12–13 as referring to the gentiles, the rustic peoples (*Forty Gospel Homilies,* pp. 319–320).

54. Cf. Matt 18:22.

55. Cf. Rev 14:1. The interpretation of the Revelation text in terms of generations is noteworthy.

56. Origen *Ex* 12.3 p. 360. Greg *Hom* 7 1101 C; 20 1162 B. The author makes a pun on the name "John" (grace). There follows a difficult passage. The key is the basic metaphor: loosening the strap of the sandal is seen as an unraveling of the mystery of the Incarnation. The foot, the lowest part of the human body, is taken to express the very depth of the Incarnation. The immediate source for this is probably the writings of Gregory the Great, but ultimately it goes back to Origen (Origen, *Commentary on the Gospel according to John,* Book 4.157, 172 pp. 213, 217; *Homilies on Genesis and Exodus,* Hom 12, p. 370). Gregory uses Ps 59:10 in this context as our commentator does. The fuller development and

part of the body. A savior, incarnate in the fullest way, is at hand to bring about righteousness. Therefore, it is said through the prophet, *I will stretch out my sandal over Idumea*.[57] Unless one is joined to the knowledge of the Spirit, no one except by means of the grace of forgiveness investigates the mystery of Christ's incarnation—how *the Word became flesh*;[58] where the flesh, where the soul, and where the spirit of Christ originate, so that he is both truly human *in every way, with the exception of sin*,[59] and true God in true God without beginning. The same one is the Son of Man who is in heaven. And how he emerged *like a bridegroom* from his chamber, that is from the virginal womb, while "leaving it closed, just as it was closed when he entered."[60]

Therefore, now that the true bridegroom has come, the house of John is called *the house of the barefoot man* who says, *Whoever has the bride is the bridegroom*.[61] For that reason, the Holy Spirit descends in the form of a dove (cf. Mark 1:10). This is the one who is serenaded in the Song of Songs: *My bride . . . my lover . . . my intimate . . . my beloved . . . my dove*.[62] The Spirit is said to be a bride in the Patriarchs, a lover in the Prophets, an intimate in the case of Joseph and Mary, a beloved in the case of John the Baptist, a dove in the case of Christ and of the apostles.[63] The apostles are told, *Be wise as serpents and simple as doves*.[64]

---

explanation of Gregory is much easier to follow than the succinct remark of our commentator (Gregory the Great, *Forty Gospel Homilies*, pp. 24–25, 38, 274–275).

57. Ps 60:8 (= 108:9). The mention of sandal in the NT leads to a text in the OT using the same term. The development of an imaginative, indeed poetic, approach to such texts is necessary to appreciate the patristic usage.

58. John 1:14.

59. Cf. Heb 4:15. The influence of Gregory's homilies on the Gospels is evident here. He stresses the difficulty of investigation of this mystery (Gregory the Great, *Forty Gospel Homilies*, p. 25).

60. Cf. Ps 119:4–5. All texts, even in the OT, using the term "bridegroom," were susceptible of this interpretation. There is a quotation here from an ancient Christian epic, the *Carmen Paschale* of Sedulius. Sedulius writes: . . . *pro virgine testis, partus adest, clausa ingrediens et clausa relinquens. Clausa* refers to *intemerata viscera*, earlier spoken of (2, p. 47, 45–47).

61. John 3:29; cf. Deut 25:10. Jerome *Math* p. 18 262–297. The original polemical context of the phrase is in sharp contrast with the self-effacing behavior of the Baptist. Sensitivity to importance of context for the interpretation of texts is not a feature of the earlier exegesis. If a phrase in itself seemed appropriate, then it was used. Recognizing the source of a text, or recognizing a quotation, helps us to understand the present commentary text, but the original context of the quotation often throws little light.

62. The elements in this string of terms of endearment are found throughout the Song of Songs, e.g., "dove" (2:14).

63. The titles are taken in turn and apportioned to different persons and periods in the Bible. The author has some established conventional linkage in mind. In the case of the story of Christ and the apostles, he explains the association, but his reasoning in the case of the rest is not clear.

64. Matt 10:16.

It continues, **I have baptized you in water, he will baptize in the Holy Spirit** (Mark 1:8).

What is the difference between the water and the Holy Spirit who *is carried over the waters?*[65] The water represents the ministry of John; the Spirit is the divine ministry. It is written: *The Spirit of God is borne over the waters.*[66] The text says "over" not "under." Just as the soul is more excellent than the body it governs, so the spirit is more excellent than the soul. But the spirit *remained over him.*[67] This is the anointing of Christ according to the flesh.[68] We read about this anointing, *Therefore God, your God, has anointed you with the oil of gladness above your fellows.*[69] Oil cannot be under water.[70] In the same way, the creator cannot be under a creature.

Oil rises up from the bitterness of the root and reaches the top as a fuel for light, medicine for wounds, and food for the hungry.[71] And in this way, the anointing of the body of Christ starts from the bitterness of the passion and reaches to the glory of the resurrection. The Apostle advises us: *Have, then, this mind in you which was in Christ Jesus*, etc., as far as *even to death, death on a cross. Therefore God exalted him and gave him a name that is above every name because the Lord Jesus is in the glory of God the Father.*[72]

And it came about in those days that Jesus came from Nazareth, etc., as far as **and he was with the beasts and the angels were ministering to him** (Mark 1:9–13).[73]

Mark the Evangelist bounds along over level and difficult places, like *a deer seeking the springs of water.*[74] He plucks only the tips of the vegetation and carries off the topmost branches. He is like a honeybee that fleetingly tastes the

65. Cf. Gen 1:2.

66. Gen 1:2.

67. John 1:32.

68. Cf. Mark 1:11. Just as Jesus undergoes Baptism, as man he now receives the sacrament of Confirmation.

69. Ps 45:7.

70. Aug *Conf* xiii, 9. The comparison of oil and water is found in St. Augustine's *Confessions* (xiii, 9) in relation to Gen 1:2.

71. The reference to the uses of olive oil for anointing suggests a Mediterranean setting for the writing. But it is possible that information gathered from study, especially biblical commentary, or from travel is being used. Would such a development on the subject of olive oil have come spontaneously to the mind of an Irish author? In the Irish way of life, the place of oil was taken by butter.

72. Phil 2:5–11.

73. Only the beginning and end of the passage are quoted; "etc., as far as" is a literal translation.

74. Cf. Ps 42:1.

flowers of the field, to which is likened the smell of Isaac.[75] Such is the way
Mark recounts how Jesus came from Nazareth in Galilee to receive baptism in
the Jordan from John;[76] as soon as he came out of the water, he saw the heavens opened, and the Spirit descending like a dove, and remaining upon him;[77]
and the voice of the Father came from heaven saying that he was pleased with
his beloved Son; and the Spirit drove him into the desert; and the temptation
by Satan for 40 days and nights; he was with the beasts, and he lingered with
the ministering angels. This order of events is to be morally followed by us
according to the example of Christ.[78] We must hasten to seek the company
of angels. Jesus demonstrated this by deed before he taught it by word. Thus
we also run with the young people after the bridegroom,[79] drawn from the
fickleness of this uncertain world of the will by the scent of the flower of
purity.[80]

And through the mysteries of baptism, from the two fountains of love, that
of God and that of neighbor, we are washed by the grace of forgiveness,[81] and
we ascend by hope and we contemplate the heavenly secrets through the eyes
of a clean heart.[82] Thereupon, *in a contrite and humbled* spirit,[83] we, with simple
heart, receive the Holy Spirit, who descends upon the meek,[84] and who *abides*,
with never-failing love.

The voice of the Lord from the heavens is directed at us who are beloved of
God, *Blessed are the peacemakers, because they shall be called children of God.*[85] Then
the Father, together with the Son and the Holy Spirit, take delight in us when
we become one spirit with God. This is why the Son makes intercession with
the Father for us, saying, *Holy Father, preserve them in your name, those whom you*

---

75. Cf. Gen 27:27.

76. The text of Mark 1:9–13 is put into indirect speech construction.

77. Cf. John 1:32 (harmonized).

78. "Example" is one of the types of Gospel material that was highlighted in the prologue. The imitation of Christ is a recurring idea in the commentary. There follows an
attempt to show how we can enter into the spirit of these opening events of Christ's life.

79. Cf. Song of Songs 1:3–4. Gregory the Great uses the text similarly (*Forty Gospel
Homilies*, p. 234).

80. The Latin has a play on words (*mundi/munditiae*).

81. I translate *sacramenta* (plural) as mysteries. This is a notoriously difficult term in early
Christian Latin, as is the term *mysteria* which we see later. The fundamental importance of
baptism is basic to the author's thought. The dual character of Christian love is more than
once underlined by the author. Both are necessary. This twofold character of love (*charitas*)
is a constant in the writings of Gregory the Great.

82. Cf. Matt 5:8.

83. Cf. Ps 51:17.

84. Cf. Matt 5:9.

85. Matt 5:9.

have given to me, so that they may be one just as we are one.[86] Then *suddenly*, the Spirit *drives* us out into the desert, for a 40-day period, to be tempted *by Satan*. This is so that our *suffering* might produce *perseverance*, perseverance *hope*, and that hope might result in charity.[87] Since *our struggle is not against flesh and blood but against the principalities*, etc.[88]

At that point, the wild beasts will be at peace with us in the ark of our soul. Let us tame the clean and unclean animals.[89] And like Daniel we sleep with lions,[90] since the *spirit* is not *against the flesh*, nor does *the flesh lust against the spirit*. Afterwards, the ministering angels, who *see the face* of our Father in heaven,[91] are always sent to us to respond to our needs and to provide solace for our expectant hearts. They announce, *Your prayer has been heard,* and *Do not fear, you who are seeking Jesus, the Nazarene,* and *I rebuke and discipline those whom I love,* and *To him who conquers I will give to eat of the tree which is in the paradise of my God.*[92]

It continues, **After John had been arrested, Jesus came into Galilee,** etc. (Mark 1:14).

Now we have received *grace for grace*.[93] Things of the flesh are beheaded, while spiritual realities are brought to life.[94] Pretence gives way; truth arrives. John is in prison—the Law is in Judea. Jesus is in Galilee—there is salvation among the gentiles.[95]

86. John 17:11, 22 compounded.
87. Cf. Rom 5:3–5.
88. Cf. Eph 6:12 with an intrusion from 1:21. Texts often appear to be misquoted. Sometimes this is due to quoting from memory, leading to similar texts being confused. Other times, texts are merged to make a convenient statement. It is difficult to establish clear distinctions between allusions, paraphrases, and carelessness.
89. Aug *Iob* p. 517 22–23; PetC *Ser* 58 p. 326 29–30; Greg *Iob* 31 p. 1551 42–43. Cf. Gen 7:1–8.
90. Cf. Dan 6:16–24.
91. Cf. Matt 18:10.
92. There follows a list of messages delivered by angels: Acts 10:31; cf. Mark 16:6; Rev 3:19; cf. Rev 2:7. This concludes the sustained allegorical treatment of Mark 1:8–13. Some of the spiritual application is not clear. Does the author mean to refer to an actual time in a "desert"? Is this a reference to a monastic discipline? In Irish monasticism such practice is well documented for a somewhat later period, as in the "Céile Dé" movement (Peter O'Dwyer, *Céli Dé: Spiritual Reform in Ireland, 750–900*).
93. Cf. John 1:16. The phrase in John 1:16 has always been difficult to understand and translate. The commentator plays on the term "grace" in relation to Mark 1:14. One "grace" (John) is taken away to be replaced by a better.
94. The beheading of John in Mark 6:28 is anticipated.
95. Judea is seen as the heartland of Judaism while Galilee is associated with the gentiles. The true meaning of the Law is regarded as imprisoned within Judaism.

Preaching the gospel of the kingdom (Mark 1:15).

Blessed are the poor in spirit because theirs is the kingdom of heaven.[96] The poor inherit the earthly kingdom. An eternal kingdom is given to the Christian poor. For this reason the Lord says, *My kingdom is not of this world.*[97] Indeed, all earthly honor is comparable to a slight *spray* of water, or to *smoke* or a dream.[98]

It continues, **Repent and believe in the gospel** (Mark 1:15).

For "unless you believe you will not understand."[99] The sweetness of the fruit makes up for the bitterness of the root. The hope of profit can make attractive the dangers of the sea. The hope of a cure lessens the pain of the medicine. Whoever desires the kernel breaks the nut. Whoever wants to adhere to eternal goodness does penance.

Four fishermen are called "those sent" (cf. Mark 1:16–20):[100] Simon and Andrew, James and John, who abandoned their nets, their father, and the boat with the hired help.[101] In this four-horse carriage we are transported to the heavens,[102] just like Elijah.[103] The first church is constructed from these four corners.[104] By means of these four Hebrew letters, that is the "tetragrammeton," the name of the Lord is known by us.

This is an example for us. We are commanded to hear the voice of the Lord when he calls;[105] and to dismiss from our minds a vice-ridden people

96. Matt 5:3.

97. John 18:36.

98. Cf. Wis 5:15.

99. Cf. Is 7:9 (LXX). St. Augustine frequently quotes this version of the text: e.g., Aug *Ser* 272 1246 l.32. The logic of the reference to understanding is not evident. The list of proverbial sayings forms an argument to validate the necessity of penance. Is the reference to sea merchants an indication of personal familiarity and thus of provenance?

100. The Latin, *missi* is translated literally; this is what "apostles" means.

101. Cf. Mark 1:16–20.

102. This image of the carriage is normally reserved for the four evangelists, linked with the "chariot" of Ezek 1.

103. Cf. 2 Kings 2:11.

104. The early church is mentioned several times in the commentary. Here the thought is close to that of Eph 2:20, where the apostles are the "foundation." The imagery here appears to be original. The four Gospels are seen as the four corners of the church in Jerome (*Math* p. 2 24–25). Similarly, Gregory the Great sees the church represented by the Ark whose four corners are the four Gospels (*Pastoral Care*, p. 87). The four apostles, being Jews, can be presented as Hebrew letters. The name "Yahweh" is a four-lettered word in Hebrew.

105. As readers will be beginning to expect by now, there follows an application to their lives. The intended readers are probably monks, given the radical and literal nature of the exhortation. Each item left behind by the four apostles is given an allegorical meaning, though not in the same sequence. The mention of Adam's leather garments is very likely triggered off by the mention of the boat, which, as we will see (at Mark 4:38), the author understands as made of hides.

and our *ancestral* home which is *foolishness* in the sight of God;[106] and to for-
get the spider's web,[107] in which the rolling of a worthless coin was holding
us, almost like midges.[108] We are to loathe the boat of our former way of
life.[109] Indeed, Adam, our father according to the flesh, is clothed with dead
skins.[110] We now lay aside the old man *with his actions*,[111] and seek to be a
new man.[112] We are clothed in *the skins of Solomon*, of which the bride boasts
of having become as *beautiful*.[113]

   The name Simon means "obedient";[114] Andrew "manly";[115] James "overthrowing";[116] and John means "grace."[117] Through these four names we are
enlisted in the army of the Lord[118]: through obedience that we may hear,
through manliness that we may fight, through overthrowing that we may persevere, and through grace that we may be safe.[119] *Unless the Lord builds the house,
in vain do its builders work.*[120] These four are said to be the cardinal virtues.[121]

   106. Cf. 1 Pet 1:18; 1 Cor 3:19.
   107. There is a pun here. The Latin *rete* can mean "net," as in the Gospel text, or "web."
The Latin has the plural "spiders."
   108. The Latin text is somewhat conjectural. The author appears to be referring to the
monks' success in overcoming worldly love of money.
   109. Cf. Eph 4:22.
   110. Cf. Gen 3:21. Euch *Form* p. 37 14. Hides or animal skins were explained by the
compiler of traditions, Eucherius, as a sign of mortality.
   111. Cf. Col 3:9.
   112. Cf. Eph 4:22–24.
   113. Cf. Song 1:5 (1:4, Vulgate). The imagery here is based on the Latin version, which
differs from the reading of the Hebrew (eliminating the reference to Solomon) preferred
by modern scholars and translators. If the parallelism with "tents" is allowed to have force,
then "hides" here also denotes tents, which were made of hides. The attractiveness of being
so clothed is not evident. The thrust of the allusion is probably to the fine robes of Solomon,
but the line of thought is very compressed.
   114. Euch *Ins* p. 143 21; Jerome *Nom* p. 151 7.
   115. Jerome *Nom* p. 142 26.
   116. Jerome *Nom* p. 67 19; p. 136 27; p. 157 5.
   117. See Mark 1:4 earlier. The meanings correspond to those given by Jerome in his
glossary.
   118. PetC *Ser* 130 bis p. 802 1.
   119. The military enlistment analogy is sustained in reference to the meaning of the
four names. The precise nuance intended is not easy to grasp in every case; for example,
why does overthrowing ensure perseverance? Perhaps it suggests that opposition must be
overthrown? Is there a clue to be determined here in regard to dating and origin? The
church had to struggle hard throughout the fifth and sixth centuries to obtain exemption
of clerics and religious from military conscription. Certainly, this was not an Irish problem.
   120. Ps 127:1.
   121. There is an awkwardness in the parallel proposed with the cardinal virtues. The
fit is not comfortable. Sometimes the demands of the established syllabus strain the capacity
of the underlying text to sustain the allegory. The writer wants to teach the importance of
the cardinal virtues, part of the pagan legacy that was early integrated into Christian moral
theology. The allegorists show remarkable ingenuity but sometimes falter.

We obey through prudence, we act in a manly way through justice, through temperance we tread upon *serpents*,[122] and through fortitude we earn the grace of God.

Due to being so busy attending to the needs of the brothers, I have been unable to explain the Evangelist Mark as I would have wished.[123] However, I imitate him by touching briefly upon the things that are proper to him. Just like Ruth, the kinswoman of the Lord, I follow the reapers, and I glean ears and stalks for the widowed Naomi. If only I could get into the company of Boaz through my poverty, by means of a praiseworthy theft![124]

Mark arranged the passages of the Gospel in view of the Gospel itself and not for their own sake. He did not follow the order of the story but followed the order of the mysteries.[125] This is why he tells the story of the first miracle as occurring on the sabbath.[126]

And they entered Capernaum on the sabbath (cf. Mark 1:21).

Capernaum is interpreted as the "town of consolation" and sabbath means "rest."[127] The man with the unclean spirit is healed through rest and consolation, that the place and time may correspond with health. The man with the

122. Cf. Luke 10:19.

123. The commentator speaks here in the unmistakable tone of the hardworking abbot-scholar, torn from his study by the demands of administration in the monastery. His apology leads to a digression about Mark's approach, which was dealt with in the prologue.

124. Cf. Ruth 2–3. PsIsid *Lib* 1292 D; *Mc* p. 220 7–8. The phrase *furtum laudabile* ("praiseworthy theft") is normally used in regard to the traditional assumption that Mark fashioned his Gospel from the content of Peter's preaching. Maura Walsh sees in the use of the phrase a probable indication of Irish authorship of the commentary because of its occurrence in other texts of probable Irish provenance. They provide a useful survey of the evidence (Maura Walsh and Dáibhí Ó Cróinín,Cummian's Letter, pp. 219–220). In the present instance, however, it seems to me that the writer is applying the phrase to describe his own work.

125. Jerome *Math* p. 2 33–34. These lines are remarkably similar to the approach of today's redaction criticism, which concentrates on the individual control of the traditional Gospel material by each evangelist. The term "mysteries" is one of the difficult words in the commentary, where it has a range of meanings. Here it suggests that a deeper spiritual sense lies hidden beneath the narrative of Jesus' doings. The etymology that follows is an example.

126. I translate *virtus* as "miracle." The commentator will draw attention to fifteen miracles ("virtutes") of Jesus in Mark. Morin suggests that the term is derived from Sedulius's introduction to his prose version of the *Carmen Paschale*, although the term does not occur as frequently as Morin asserts ("Un commentaire romain," p. 355; the Sedulius connection was very important for Morin's early-fifth-century dating proposal). Adomnan's uses the term "virtutes" for the wonders reported of Columcille. The miracle at Cana is referred to as *primam virtutem* in the *Catechesis Celtica* (p. 73, 1.47).

127. Jerome *Nom* p. 139 12; p. 157 14.

unclean spirit stands for the human race.[128] Uncleanliness reigned in the human race *from Adam to Moses.* For *those who sinned without the Law* perished *without the Law.*[129] The spirit recognizes *the Holy One of God* and is ordered to be quiet, while there were some who recognized God but *did not glorify him as God.*[130] *They served the creature instead of the creator.*[131]

The spirit convulsed the man and went out of him (cf. Mark 1:26). Salvation draws near, trial approaches. Pharaoh, once he is abandoned by Israel, persecutes Israel.[132] The devil scorned is a devil who hastens to bring people down.[133]

The second miracle takes place when he takes the fever ridden mother-in-law of Peter by the hand, lifts her up and she is healed. The fever stands for intemperance. We, the children of the synagogue, are healed of this by the hand of discipline, and the elevation of our desire. And we serve the one who heals us at the evening time of a will which deviates from us.[134]

And the whole city was gathered at the door and he healed many from various ailments (Mark 1:33–34).

Morally speaking, the door of the kingdom is repentance, along with faith which brings about the cure from various ailments. For the city of the world is enfeebled by many vices.[135]

---

128. Using a character as an image for the human race is common in Gregory. The generations from Adam to Christ were earlier described as "wretches." Here the span reaches only to Moses (cf. Rom 5:14), possibly because of the synagogue setting, but it is not clear why the pre-Mosaic period is highlighted, in that the man healed was also Jewish.

129. Cf. Rom 2:12.

130. Rom 1:21.

131. Cf. Rom 1:21.

132. Cf. Ex 14.

133. The commentary here represents in miniature the technique of the author. He recognizes a principle, which he illustrates from the OT (Ex 14:5ff), and then he draws a lesson for the situation of the believer today.

134. Each element of the story is given an allegorical interpretation. Intemperance is the vice selected for treatment. Christians are reminded that they are spiritually descended from the Jews, though this is a somewhat backhanded compliment: The attitude of the commentator to the Jews is complex. The Latin of this sentence is not easy to understand; I give a very literal translation. The allegorical handling of the serving is combined unclearly with that of the healings in Mark 1:32. There may be an allusion here to the advanced age of the author himself, or possibly he is thinking of the world as coming to an end, an idea found in Gregory the Great, among others.

135. C. Arles *Ser* 115 p. 480 5; 151 p. 618 1–2. The importance of penance is stressed repeatedly. The term "morally" could refer to the moral (i.e., spiritual) sense of the text or to a principle of asceticism. The sick represent the moral state of the world. The view of the world evidenced in the commentary is pessimistic.

That is why the leper is cleansed (cf. Mark 1:40), and this is the third miracle. On bended knee he begged the will of the Lord, who does not will the death of the sinner but that he be converted and live.[136] Our leprosy is the sin of the first man. This leprosy began from the head when he desired the kingdoms of the world.[137] *For greed is the root of all evils.*[138] Thus, Gehazi pursued the painted ladies, and he was affected with leprosy.[139] Once this is shown to the true priest who offers according to the order of Melchizedek,[140] it is cleansed by the gift. This true priest says, *Give alms and all things are clean for you.*[141]

The text continues and it is one of the passages proper to Mark.[142] That is, Jesus could not openly enter a city, **but he was out in desert places, and they came to him from everywhere** (cf. Mark 1:45).

Certainly Jesus was not made known to all those who in wide-open places serve their own praises and wishes.[143] However, he does show himself to those who, like Peter, go out into the desert places which the Lord chose for prayer and for feeding the people,[144] who forsake the love of the world and who give up everything they possess, so that they may say, *The Lord is my inheritance.*[145] Indeed the glory of the Lord is made known among those who assemble from all over, that is to say, through rough and smooth, those who do not find anything that may separate them *from the love of Christ.*[146]

---

136. Cf. Ezek 18:23. The switch to the OT text, which does not deal with leprosy, is easily done when leprosy is presented as an image of sin, as in the following lines.

137. Cf. Matt 4:8 (?); Greg *Reg* p. 170 83–106.

138. 1 Tim 6:10.

139. Cf. 2 Kings 5:20–27. The transition to Gehazi the leper could have been made directly. But an opportunity to condemn another vice, greed, is availed of. Gregory links avarice with skin disease in his *Pastoral Care* (pp. 43–44, where he refers to 1 Tim 6:10). Cf. C. Arles *Ser* 129 p. 531 no. 509. There is difficulty establishing the Latin text here. I have taken the reading "painted females (ladies)" as an allusion to the maidservants of 2 Kings 5:27; Jerome uses the same term *gypseas* to speak disparagingly of women who "plaster" their faces.

140. Cf. Heb 5:10.

141. Luke 11:41.

142. The commentator says in the prologue that he will pay special attention to the sections proper to Mark, although subsequently he concedes that he will imitate Mark in his brevity.

143. This appears to be an allusion to the attack of Jesus on those who parade their good deeds in public (e.g., Matt 6:5).

144. Cf. Mark 1:36. Also this is perhaps an allusion to Peter's going out to weep, in Luke 22:62. This is taken as a model for all those who need to go out to meet the Lord. Cf. Mark 6:31–44 par.

145. Ps 119:57.

146. Cf. Rom 8:35a.

CHAPTER 2

Next, we have the fourth miracle.[1] Four men come carrying *the paralytic* on a stretcher (cf. Mark 2:3). They are impeded by the crowd so they remove the roof. Through their faith the paralytic is forgiven his sins. He carries the bed on which he was carried, and he goes home in the sight of everyone. Moreover, his paralysis serves as a type for the time when he lies in the softness of the flesh, though having the desire for salvation. He is impeded by the crowds of sloth, and by indecisive thoughts which are like useless legs. The four who carry him are those we termed virtues above. They bring him to the roof tiles of divinity and wisdom exposed in Christ's fleshly house.[2] He is told, as a obligation, to carry the flesh which used to carry him.[3]

---

1. What we call the second chapter of Mark's Gospel gets short shrift from the commentator. It is not clear why he comments only on the two opening incidents. The reason cannot be his declared intention to concentrate on parts proper to Mark because all of Mark 2 is paralleled in Matthew and Luke. It is worth recalling that the writer, along with the other ancient commentators, did not read the Gospel in our modern chapter and verse divisions. These have no critical significance and should not be allowed to influence our perception of the movement of the narrative.

2. It is hard not to be captivated by the charm of this interpretation, although the method is not acceptable today. The primary goal of such commentary is to instruct and edify. The doctrines of the Incarnation, the divinity, and the humanity of Christ are major ones, so opportunities to call them to mind and illustrate them are seized upon.

3. This is puzzling. In the Gospel text he is told to carry the bed not "the flesh." The bed can certainly be seen as something that used to carry him. The commentary text has "to carry the flesh." Despite the agreement of all the manuscripts, it is likely that there is a

This was so that he may return to his own place *by another way*, like the Magi.[4]

After this, Levi, son of Alpheus is called (cf. Mark 2:14). Levi means "placed near."[5] From the tax office of worldly business he follows only the Word who says, *Whoever will not renounce all he possesses cannot be my disciple.*[6]

---

simple error here; perhaps the writer was distracted and used the wrong word. The author clearly wants to suggest the necessity of a change of behavior, expressed in terms of the man controlling the flesh and not vice versa.

4. Cf. Matt 2:12. Greg *Hom* 10 1113 C–D. Gregory the Great in his homily on Matt 2:1–2 similarly uses the phrase "by another way": we must return to the lost paradise by another way, "in bitter anger at our sins" (*Forty Gospel Homilies*, pp. 59–60). This may have inspired the present usage.

5. Jerome, *Nom* p. 140 5.

6. Luke 14:33.

CHAPTER 3

The fifth miracle: There was a man with a withered hand. To him it is said, **Stretch out your hand** (Mark 3:1).

He represents the misers who have no wish *to give* but who only want *to receive.*[1] They want to grasp and not distribute. They are told to stretch out their hands. In other words, *the thief must no longer steal. Rather he must labor, making an effort to do good with his own hands, so that he might have something* to share with the poor.[2]

And going up on the mountain, he called to him those whom he wanted, etc., as far as **who betrayed him** (Mark 3:13–19).[3]

They are called on a mountain, that is to say, those who are eminent in merit and in word, so that the place should correspond with such lofty merits.

That is, **that the twelve might be with him** (Mark 3:14).

---

1. Cf. Acts 20:35.

2. Cf. Mark 3:16; cf. Eph 4:28. This is a remarkable example of an inconsistency between the allegorical interpretation of a story and the literal-historical sense. Ideally, the latter was to be respected and serve as anchor and guide for the allegorical. Although the man stretches out his hand on Christ's instructions and is enabled to do so because of Christ's miraculous cure, nevertheless he is presented as an example of a miser. Then the stretching is taken in another sense, as the act of working. Each of the different senses ignores the intrinsic sense of the healing as the restoration of the man's well-being.

3. The opening and closing words identify the pericope for treatment. Specific parts within this section will be cited as necessary.

The Lord loved *the beauty of Jacob*[4] and when the Most High divided the peoples and split up the children of Adam, *he established limits for the peoples according to the number of the sons of Israel.*[5] This was so that they might sit upon twelve thrones *judging the twelve tribes of Israel.*[6] To them was given the power which the Son received from the Father according to the flesh.[7] In this way they themselves might do *the works* he did, and *greater than these* would they do.[8]

And he conferred the name Peter on Simon (Mark 3:16).

From "obedience" he ascends to "recognition."[9] *For whoever has, to him will it be given and he will abound.*[10]

Then James, who has overthrown all the *desires of the flesh,*[11] and John, who by grace receives what others get through effort.[12]

He conferred on them the name "Boanerges," which is "sons of thunder" (Mark 3:17).

The sublime merit of these three made them worthy to hear on the mountain *the thunder* of the Father sounding through the cloud about his Son, *This is my beloved son.*[13] This happened so that through the cloud of the flesh, they

---

4. Cf. Ps 47:4.

5. Deut 32:8.

6. Cf. Matt 19:28.

7. Jacob had 12 sons (Gen 35:22–26) who were regarded as the fathers of the 12 tribes of Israel (Gen 49:28). Cf. Deut 32:8 according to the Vulgate, which follows the Hebrew here. The coherence of this passage is hard to determine. Matt 19:28 (and parallels) has the apostles judging the tribes. They are seen as sharing in the power of Jesus. Note the qualification "according to the flesh," which the Arian heresy had made necessary, since they saw the Son as subordinate to the Father. The commentator points out that any limits of Jesus pertain to his human nature.

8. Cf. John 14:12.

9. Jerome *Nom* p. 141 18; p. 151 7; Euch *Ins* p. 143 21. Etymology is used to offer a spiritual message, though in some cases the meanings proposed are enigmatic. Maura Walsh and Dáibhí Ó Cróinín note that the order of names followed is not "distinctively Irish" (*Cummian's Letter*, p. 221). However, it should be observed that the author is following the sequence of the Gospel text. The author uses the etymologies to draw a lesson, such as obedience will bring about blessing. For most of the names listed here, there is correspondence with Jerome's glossary, but the information was also available in Eucherius, who is used very often by the commentator.

10. Matt 13:12.

11. Cf. Gal 5:16. Jerome *Nom* p. 67 19; p. 136 27; p. 157 5.

12. Jerome *Nom* p. 146 16–17; p. 155 19.

13. Matt 16:5; cf. John 12:28–29.

themselves, too, would scatter the *fire* of the word like flashes of lightning that turn into rain upon the earth.[14] Because *God has made lightning turn into rain, so that mercy might extinguish what judgment burns by fire.*[15] As the prophet says, *Mercy and judgment I will sing to you, Lord.*[16]

And **Andrew** (Mark 3:18), whose manly form[17] forced him to his destruction, so that he has the response of death within himself always,[18] and so that he has his life in his hands always.[19]

And **Philip,** which means "the mouth of the lamp."[20] He is able to illumine with his mouth what he has conceived in his heart. The Lord has given him the opening of an illuminated mouth.

And **Bartholomew,** which means "son of the one who holds up the waters."[21] And who is "the one holding up the waters" if not he who said, *And I will order the clouds not to shed rain upon it?*[22] The name *sons of God* is acquired through peace and through love of enemy. *Blessed are the peacemakers because they are the sons of God,*[23] and *Love your enemies so that you may be sons of God,* etc.[24]

And **Matthew,** which means "given."[25] The Lord granted him the gift not only of remission of sins but of enrollment among the number of apostles, in order that *the lion and the ox* may eat together, and *the wolf* may feed with *the lamb.*[26]

---

14. Cf. Luke 12:49.

15. Ps 135:7.

16. The imagery is used to remind readers that God acts through human ministry. As Jesus casts fire upon the earth (Luke 12:49), so the apostles. The remark about the cloud, thunder, and lightning leads to the use of an OT text, Ps 135:7, leading to the quotation of Ps 101:1.

17. Jerome *Nom* p. 142 26; Euch *Ins* p. 143 25.

18. Cf. 2 Cor 1:9.

19. Cf. Ps 119:109.

20. Jerome *Nom* p. 140 22–23.

21. Jerome *Nom* p. 135 20.

22. Is 5:6.

23. Matt 5:9.

24. Matt 5:44–45.

25. Jerome *Nom* p. 147 1.

26. Cf. Is 65:25. This appears to be a reference to the diverse backgrounds of the twelve. Possibly Matthew is viewed as a collaborator with the Romans and a renegade Jew.

And **Thomas,** which means "abyss."[27] For many know *the deep things of God* but say little;[28] as Paul says, *I know a man*, etc., as far as, *may not be spoken by any human being*.[29]

And **James, son of Alphaeus,** means "son of the instructed one,"[30] or "son of the thousandth."[31] At his side *a thousand* fall and at his right hand, *ten thousand*.[32] He is another Jacob whose struggle is not *against flesh and blood but against spiritual evils*.[33]

And **Thaddaeus,** which means "little heart,"[34] that is to say, a cultivator of the heart. He preserves his heart *with every means of protection*.[35] By purity of heart God is seen, just as in a *clean mirror* an image is clearly shown.[36]

And **Simon the Cananean** who was also a Zealot.[37] Simon means "dismissing melancholy."[38] For *blessed are those who mourn* now, *because they will be consoled*.[39] The person who seeks future consolation has to realize a threefold sorrow: weep copiously for his own sins with David and Mary; weep with those who weep, along with Paul; and weep much with John who said, *and I wept much because there was no one found worthy to open the book* and *to break its seals*.[40] He is called a Zealot because *zeal for the Lord's house consumes*.[41] This is how Phinehas the priest behaved so that the plague might cease.[42]

27. Jerome *Nom* p. 149 7.
28. Cf. 1 Cor 2:10.
29. Cf. 2 Cor 12:2–4.
30. This meaning is not found in Jerome or in Eucherius.
31. Jerome *Nom* p. 134 16.
32. Cf. Ps 91:7.
33. The linking of James with Jacob's struggle (Gen 32:24–32) is easily made because in Latin the names are the same. The further association with Eph 6:12 is somewhat strained because Jacob's adversary is not simply an evil force.
34. Euch *Ins* p. 144 4–5.
35. Cf. Prov 4:23.
36. Cf. Matt 5:8; Rev 21:18, 21. Jerome does not have this name and explanation in his glossary, but they are found in Eucherius.
37. Cf. Luke 6:15.
38. Jerome *Nom* p. 141 1–2; Euch *Ins* p. 143 20.
39. Cf. Matt 5:5.
40. A development follows on the ways to be sorrowful in the present, so as to ensure future happiness. Biblical examples are given: cf. 2 Kings 12:13ff (cf. title of Ps 51); Luke 7:38 (the tradition identified the woman as Mary); cf. Rom 12:5; Rev 5:2, 4 (compressed).
41. Cf. Ps 69:9; cf. John 2:17.
42. Zealot is not so explained in Jerome and Eucherius. Cf. Num 25:7–9; Ps 106:30.

And **Judas Iscariot** who betrayed him (Mark 3:19). He does not wipe away his sin through repentance, nor is the sin ever wiped from God's memory. For this reason it is said of him, *May his mother's sin not be wiped out*; may it be *before the Lord always*.[43] Judas means either "confessing" or "boastful."[44] Iscariot means the "memory of death."[45] There are many proud and boastful confessors in the church. Foremost are Simon Magus[46] and Arius and the other heretics whose memory is deadly. Thus it is celebrated in the church so that it may be avoided.[47]

These are the twelve different types of apostles and preachers, who, in four groups of three, keep watch around the tabernacle of the Lord.[48] They *carry* the holy words of the Lord on their own *shoulders* of works,[49] as they carry the one tabernacle *with many abodes*[50] to the *promised land*.[51]

The example of one preserves them in humble fear, just as the fall of the infamous Lucifer does for the angels. *Let the wise man not be conceited in his wisdom*, but *let him who boasts, boast in the Lord*.[52]

It continues: **And they came home,** etc., as far as **he is out of his mind** (Mark 3:20–21).

Mark is the only one to tell the story of Jesus coming home with his disciples.[53] He records that *again* crowds gathered *so that they could not eat bread*, and that the disciples thought that he had gone *out of his mind*. For the scribes who had come from Jerusalem said, *Beelzebub is in him* (Mark 3:22). *As high as*

---

43. Ps 109:14b–15a.

44. Jerome *Nom* p. 136 27–28.

45. Jerome *Nom* p. 137 2.

46. Cf. Acts 8:9–24.

47. Cf. Titus 3:10. The three meanings proposed (following Jerome) are ingeniously combined to allow a condemnation of Simon Magus (Acts 8:9–24) and Arius (c. 250–c. 336). Mention of heretics, especially Arius, is a feature of writings of this period. Europe was divided between Arian and Catholic Christians for about 200 years, the time preceding this commentary, if the date of early-seventh-century composition is accepted. For example, the part of Europe evangelized by Columbanus was strongly influenced by Arianism.

48. Cf. Num 1:50 (cf. Num 1–3).

49. Cf. Num 1:50.

50. Cf. John 14:2.

51. Cf. Heb 11:9. The imagery here is taken from the camp arrangements for the 12 tribes outlined in Num 2, and the duties of the Levites described in Num 4. The Ten Commandments were carried inside the Ark. The twelve apostles are seen as carrying the church to heaven, as the Levites carried the ark to the Promised Land. Eucherius explains the tabernacle as the church (Euch *Form* p. 51).

52. Cf. Luke 10:18; Jer 9:22; 1 Cor 1:31.

53. The commentator promises in his prologue to attend especially to sections proper to Mark. Here he draws attention to such a passage, but merely paraphrases it slightly.

the heavens are above the earth, so are the ways of the Lord higher than ours.[54] Indeed, *for this* he came.[55] Because he has heard and he suffers, he who says to us, *Blessed* will you be *when people curse you*, etc., as far as, *your reward in heaven.*[56]

The home they come to is the early church. The crowds which stop them from eating bread are sins and vices,[57] for whoever eats *unworthily, eats and drinks to his own condemnation, not discerning the body* of the Lord.[58] Therefore the Lord is in a rage, saying, *Unless you eat the flesh of the Son of Man*, etc., as far as, *you will not have life in you.*[59]

And whoever sins against the Holy Spirit does not get forgiveness but is guilty of an eternal sin (Mark 3:29).

Because he does not deserve to practice repentance in order to become acceptable who, knowing Christ, says that he is the prince of demons.[60] Because he will never be released from prison who has not paid for every *last quarter* of a word before the end of life.[61] The coin of eternal life is made up, in fact, of four quarters[62]: You must confess with your *mouth* what you believe in your *heart*;[63] you must put into practice what you confess; you must not cease to teach what you practice; for *whoever will do and will teach, will be called great in the kingdom of heaven.*[64]

And his mother and his brothers come (Mark 3:31).

So that we may know that we are his brothers and his mother, if we do the will of his Father. In this way we become *coheirs* with him who judges not according to gender but according to deeds.[65]

---

54. Cf. Is 55:9 (with 9b accommodated).

55. Cf. John 18:37.

56. The insult of the Scribes is explained by the inability of the human mind to understand the actions of God. Jesus suffered because of this, and so his beatitude saying (Matt 5:11–12) can be said to be based on his own experience.

57. As the impeding crowds in Mark 2:4 are interpreted as sloth, so here the troublesome crowds are seen as vices.

58. Cf. 1 Cor 11:29.

59. Cf. 1 Cor 11:27, 29. The author imagines Jesus in a rage over the abuse Paul is talking about and reacting with the declaration of John 6:53.

60. The author equates the sin against the Holy Spirit with the insult of the Scribes.

61. Cf. Matt 5:26; 18:30, 34.

62. The commentator uses currency metaphors. It is notoriously difficult to find modern equivalencies for translation purposes. The Latin has *quadrantem verbi novissimum* ("the very last quarter of a word"); *quattuor partibus denarius* ("a denarius made up of four parts").

63. Cf. Rom 10:9.

64. Matt 5:19b.

65. Cf. Rom 8:17.

CHAPTER 4

❦

Then, **he began to teach by the seashore** (Mark 4:1).

He did this so that the place where the teaching took place might indicate that the listeners were bitter and fickle.[1] Therefore, he speaks to them in parables so that they might seek what they did not understand and that, through the apostles whom they despised,[2] they might learn the mystery of the kingdom which they themselves did not possess.[3]

The image of a yield of 30-, 60-, and 100-fold represents the Law, Prophecy and the Gospel (cf. Mark 4:8). In this way, in the mouth of the three witnesses, namely Moses and Elijah, and Jesus, the mystery of the kingdom revealed on the mountain is confirmed.[4]

---

1. The commentator proceeds from a consideration of the literal sense to an allegorical meaning. In Latin *mare* ("sea") suggests *amarus* ("bitter"). However, his knowledge of geography is faulty since the water of the Sea of Galilee is fresh. It is possible, of course, that he knew this but was overcome by the spiritual benefits of the allegory. The Irish in Iona in the late seventh century knew that the Sea of Galilee had fresh water. In Adomnan's *De Locis Sanctis* we read: *cujus aquae dulces et ad potandum habiles* ("the waters of which are sweet and suitable for drinking"; no. 20, p. 91).

2. Cf. 1 Cor 6:4.

3. The author jumps to Mark 4:11–12, where Jesus contrasts the apostles' knowledge with those "outside." The issue of the despising of the apostles is not found in the text.

4. Cf. 1 John 5:7–8. The commentator offers only a brief mention of the parable of the sower (Mark 4:3–19) and its explanation (Mark 4:13–20). Law, prophecy, and gospel are seen as a crescendo of revelation and are represented in terms of the transfiguration (Mark 9:2–8, par).

And he said to them, "Is a lamp brought in to be put under a measure, etc., as far as **will be taken from him"** (Mark 4:21–25).

The lamp is the word about the three types of seeds. The measure, or the bed, represents the hearing of disobedient folk. The apostles whom the hidden and concealed word of God enlightens are the lampstand. The parable concerns each kind of seed. It becomes clear when the Lord treats of it.[5]

And he said, "According to the measure you have used, will you be repaid," etc. (Mark 4:24).

For indeed an understanding of the mysteries is allotted according to the measure of each one's faith, and the understanding will be increased according as virtues are added to knowledge.

For whoever has, it will be given to him (Mark 4:25).[6]

This means that whoever has faith will have virtue. Whoever has the task of preaching will have the understanding of the mystery. On the other hand, whoever does not have faith will lack virtue. And whoever does not have the task of preaching lacks understanding. Whoever does not understand, has already lost what he heard, as if he had not heard it.

And he said, "The kingdom of God is as if a man sowed seed in the ground, etc., as far as **the harvest has come"** (Mark 4:26–29).

Mark is the only evangelist to take up this next parable of the preacher.[7] The kingdom of God is the church which is ruled by God and which in turn rules humanity.[8] The church stamps on opposing forces and vices, like the centurion who has *soldiers* under his command. The man sowing the seed is the Son of Man, the seed is the word of life, and the soil is the hearts of the people. The sleep of the man represents the death of the Savior. The seed sprouts

5. The author contends that the parable of the lamp was intended by Christ as an explanation of the sower parable. We have a complex interpenetration of levels of commentary here, one parable used to present an allegorical interpretation of another.

6. The precise form of this saying of Christ is distinctively Markan (cf. Matt 7:2). The author does not advert to this, but interprets it in context, in relation to the understanding of mystery and parable.

7. The commentator draws attention to a passage proper to Mark and gives what is his fullest treatment of such material.

8. Cf. Matt 8:9. This is a very loaded sentence, involving a certain understanding of the kingdom, church, and world. The author takes a firm position. The view is similar to that found in Gregory's writings. Gregory the Great teaches that sometimes the phrase "kingdom of God" is to be taken to refer to the earthly church (e.g., *Hom* 32 1236 D; 38 1282 D; *Forty Gospel Homilies*, pp. 263, 340).

by night and day. After the sleep of Christ, *the number of believers* kept growing in faith, and increased in activity more and more, through difficult and favorable times.[9]

Though he is unaware (Mark 4:27).

This means that he prevents us from knowing who will bear fruit in the end, since whoever perseveres to the end will be saved.[10]

For the ground produces of itself (Mark 4:28).

While God awaits our will, as he says, "If you wish to come to life, *keep the commandments.*"[11]

First, the stalk (Mark 4:28).

That is, fear. "*The beginning of wisdom, the fear of the Lord.*[12]

Then, the ear (Mark 4:28).

That is, tearful repentance.

Finally, the fully developed grain in the ear (Mark 4:28), that is charity, since charity is the *fullness* of the *law*.[13]

And when the crop has appeared, he at once puts in the sickle (Mark 4:29).

The sickle stands for death or for the judgment which cuts through everything.

Since the harvest is here (Mark 4:29).

That is, the end of the age, when the righteous who sowed in tears will rejoice.[14]

Again, he compares this seed to a grain of mustard seed (cf. Mark 4:30). It is the smallest in fear, but it is the greatest in love. It is greater than *all the shrubs* (Mark 4:32). Because *God is love*; and *All flesh is grass*, and whoever is *weak*, let him eat vegetables. The shrub has put out *branches*, branches of mercy and

---

9. Cf., e.g., Acts 6:7; 11:21.
10. Cf. Matt 10:22b.
11. Cf. Matt 19:17.
12. Ps 111:10.
13. Cf. Rom 13:10.
14. The prologue concludes in similar vein.

compassion, *in whose shade* the poor of Christ, who are heavenly *animals*, are delighted to dwell.[15]

He explained everything to his disciples when they were by themselves (Mark 4:34).

For they were worthy to hear the mysteries in the innermost sanctuary of wisdom, who resided in virtuous solitude, far away from the disturbances of evil thoughts. The wisdom of the scholar is attained in leisure.[16] From there they come to the sea and are upset by the waves.

And he was in the stern, asleep on the cushion (Mark 4:38).

The boat, made of dead skins, contains living beings.[17] It holds off the waves and is strengthened with wood, that is to say, the church is saved by the cross and death of the Lord. The cushion represents the body of the Lord, on which

15. This passage is a very compressed sequence of thought and association. It reads like jottings intended for further expansion. The relative smallness and greatness of the mustard seed and mustard bush are allegorized (without attention paid to the botanical problem—the bush is not big). Three texts are then simply cited in sequence. The following reading seems reasonable. A person with love shares in the immensity of God, because God is love (1 John 4:8b). The seed/shrub is "grass" (Is 40:6), i.e., transitory, just like human life. This refers to the reverential fear represented by the smallness of the seed. The term *holus* ("vegetable"), used in Mark 4:32, is also used in Rom 14:2, cited here, but to what purpose? The phrase in Mark is a conflation and partial quotation of Dan 4:9 and 18. The Vulgate reads: *subter eam habitabant animalia et bestiae* (v. 9); *in ramis ejus commorantes aves caeli* (v. 18). This partially explains the strange description of the poor of Christ as "animals of heaven," and it shows that the author (or a source) referred to the book of Daniel as well as to the beatitude in Matt 5:3. Similar imagery is found in C. Arles *Ser* 27 p. 119 28–42; p. 121 14–16; Greg *Reg* p. 278.

16. Cf. Sir 38:45.

17. This allegorical analysis of the boat contains what the eminent German scholar Bernhard Bischoff regarded as an indication of Irish authorship. The boat described here resembles the "currach" still in use on the west coast of Ireland (Bernhard Bischoff, "Turning-Points," p. 81). For a negative reaction to Bischoff's opinion, see Edmondo Coccia, "La cultura irlandese precarolingia," pp. 344–345. At Mark 1:20 I drew attention to the mention of Adam's skin clothing; this is probably due to association with the boat being thought of as made of hides. Why does the author, Irish or not, choose to imagine the boat as a "currach"? Possibly because it was the kind that he was most familiar with due to his upbringing in an area where such boats were normal, or because he had traveled in one, coming from Ireland to Europe possibly. Bede, in his comment on Acts 27:16, writes: "A skiff or catascopos is a light boat constructed of withes and covered with untanned hide" (Bede, *Commentary on Acts*, p. 188). The translator, Lawrence Martin, notes that Bede took this from Isidore and that he subsequently qualified this explanation in his "Retractiones" (ibid., p. 191). Isidore was roughly the contemporary of the commentator on Mark (if the first half of the seventh century is accepted as the probable date). He writes in his *Etymologiae* (19.1,21) of Saxon pirates using leather-covered skiffs. Dependence on Isidore is not necessary. Both witness to a widespread knowledge of this type of boat. Also, it needs to be

divinity was bowed down like the head.[18] The boat is the church at its beginning when Jesus sleeps in a bodily sense, because *he never sleeps who guards Israel*.[19] He rebukes the wind and the sea that it may be quiet. Concerning this, it is said, *You control the might of the sea*, etc.[20] The wind and the sea are the demons and the persecutors. He says, *Be quiet* (Mark 4:39), when he restrains the edicts of wicked kings as he wishes, because it is not for a human being to direct his own steps.[21] The great calm is the church at peace after trials, or else it suggests the contemplative life after a life of activity.[22]

---

noticed that a boat larger than a coracle is required here. Though the Gospels do not specify the number of disciples, it is reasonable to suppose that the author imagined Jesus in a boat large enough to accommodate Jesus with at least the Twelve. The Irish "currach" could do so.

Attention to the historical allusion should not distract from the point the author intended to make, namely, that the hides or leather point to mortality. Gregory uses the fact that leather is made of the skin of dead animals in various ways: Christ was shod in sandals, representing the divinity assuming the dead flesh of our condition (*Hom* 7 1101 C; 17 1141 A; 22 1180 D; *Forty Gospel Homilies*, p. 24; sandals are dead skins and denote foolish words (ibid. p. 137); sandals represent the ancient fathers (ibid., p. 173).

18. The head representing the divine is found in Gregory. Gregory takes the feet to represent the Incarnation and the head as the divinity, referring to 1 Cor 11:3: "The head of Christ is God" (*Hom* 33 1243 B; *Forty Gospel Homilies*, p. 274).

19. Cf. Ps 121:4.

20. Ps 89:9.

21. Cf. Prov 16:9.

22. The allegorical reading of the story of the calming of the storm continues. The sleep of Christ does not touch his divinity, which is presented as stooping down in a manner reminiscent of the "divine condescension" of the Greek Fathers. The Psalm verse extolling the Creator God is invoked. The triple reference to persecutors, wicked kings, and trials may refer to the actual experience of the author (shades of Columbanus!) or may be simply an allusion to the lessons of church history.

The contrast of active and contemplative lives is mentioned again in relation to Mark 16:11. This technical vocabulary for different forms of the Christian life is found well established in the writings of Gregory the Great. In the middle of the fifth century, Eucherius wrote in terms of *practica* and *theoretica*, or *actualis* and *contemplativa* (Eucherius, preface to *Formulae*, p. 5).

CHAPTER 5

And immediately as he left the boat, a man from the tombs, with an unclean spirit, met him (Mark 5:2).

By the sixth miracle the man *who used to live among the tombs* is cured (Mark 5:3).[1] He was not bound in chains nor fetters, for no one could control him.

He was in the hills and among the tombs, shouting, and cutting himself with stones (Mark 5:5).

He represents the most hopeless people of the gentiles,[2] whom the Apostle describes in turn as proud,[3] boastful,[4] unclean, bloody, idolatrous, shameful, unfettered by either the law of nature or of God, or by any human fear.[5]

His *name* is *Legion* (Mark 5:9), that is the *ten thousand* who fall at the Father's right hand which is Christ.[6] *The herd of pigs* is consigned to this demon, for

---

1. The commentator continues his enumeration of the miracles of Jesus.
2. Cf. Eph 4:17–19.
3. Cf. Rom 1:30.
4. Cf. Rom 1:29; cf. 2 Tim 3:2.
5. Cf. Rom 2:14–15. The region of the Decapolis is correctly recognized as non-Jewish territory, allowing the possessed man to be easily allegorized as the gentile people. However, as we will see later, the commentator is not limited by ethnic origins in his making of allegories.
6. Cf. Ps 91:7. The same verse is used at Mark 3:18 as part of the etymological treatment of "Alphaeus." Here the casting of the large number of demons into the sea by Jesus suggests the verse to the writer and allows him to explain that, since Jesus is the right hand of the Father, he shares his power. The Roman legion did not comprise 10,000 soldiers.

whom nothing is of use except only death, as they are at once drowned with no consideration of mercy in the abyss, that is in hell, through the onset of an unexpected death. Their many herdsmen fled from them. When a fool is thrashed a wise person grows in understanding.[7]

They beseech Jesus to quit their territory just as Peter says, *Depart from me, Lord, because I am unclean.*[8] They do not want to touch the ark of God, as Uzzah did.[9] The healed man is sent home and he preaches *in the Decapolis* (Mark 5:19), while the Jews, who esteem only the letter of the Decalogue, turn away from where Roman rule was in force at that time.[10]

After these things, *Jairus* comes (cf. Mark 5:22). He is the leader of the synagogue. Because once *all the gentiles* have come in, then *all Israel* will be *saved.*[11] Jairus means "illuminating" or "illuminated."[12] This suggests that the Jewish people, with the shadow of the letter set aside, becomes, with the Spirit, both enlightened and illuminating. Falling at the feet of the Word, that is humbling himself before the incarnation of Jesus, he intercedes on behalf of the daughter. He who is life itself,[13] now enables others to live. Abraham, Moses and Samuel intercede for a dead people,[14] and Jesus accedes to their prayers.[15]

The raising of the dead girl is the seventh miracle. But along the way a woman with a hemorrhage touched *the fringe* of his garment from behind.[16] She had lost, along with health, all her wealth, wasted on useless doctors. The Lord *rested from all his labors* on the seventh day.[17] Indoors, the dead girl is raised up while, outdoors among the crowds, the half-alive woman is restored.[18] A hemorrhage

---

7. Cf. Prov 19:25.
8. Cf. Luke 5:8.
9. Cf. 2 Sam 6:6–7. The Ark was described as "the body of Christ" at Mark 1:5. Here a similar parallel is evoked.
10. Euch *Ins* p. 152 10; *Form* p. 60 16.
11. Rom 11:25.
12. Jerome *Nom* p. 140 2–3.
13. Literally, "He who lives for/to himself" (Latin: *qui sibi vivit*).
14. Cf. Gen 18; Ex 34:9; 1 Sam 7:5.
15. Origen *Jos* 16 p. 366; 26 p. 498; Greg *Hom* 27 1209 B–C; Hil *Matt* 9:5, p. 208. Jairus is efficacious in his prayer, as were his predecessors. That the prayers of OT times had value is recognized by such as Origen (see the editor's note in Origen, *Homélies sur Josué*, p. 499). Gregory the Great comments on Jer 15:1: "Why is it that Moses and Samuel are preferred to all other fathers in this matter of making requests. . . ?" (*Forty Gospel Homilies*, p. 218). The girl represents the Jewish people.
16. Mark 5:27 combined with Matt 9:20. The detail of the "fringe" is not in Mark's text.
17. Cf. Gen 2:2 and Heb 4:4. Apart from the word association with "seventh," it is difficult to situate this remark.
18. The girl (inside) and woman (outside) represent the Jews and gentiles respectively.

results in sterility and this is why the church of the gentiles is told, *Rejoice, sterile woman, you who have not given birth.*[19]

She approaches from behind, that is after the resurrection.[20] She touches the fringe, as if it were the cymbals and pomegranate-shaped decorations which hung from the hem of the high priest's tunic. A cymbal stands for confession and a pomegranate for unity.[21]

The girl is told, *tabitha cumin* (Mark 5:41), that is "rise up, girl." The leader of the synagogue is told, *Your daughter is dead* (Mark 5:35). However, Jesus said, *she is not dead but she is asleep* (Mark 5:39). Both are true: "she is dead to you, but to me she is asleep." The girl was twelve years old and the woman had been stricken for twelve years. The sins of unbelievers become obvious, once they begin to be believers. As it is said, *Abraham believed God and it was reckoned to him as righteousness.*[22]

19. Is 54:1 is cited fully in Gal 4:27, referring to the gentile church.

20. Jerome *Math* p. 59 1375. She represents the gentiles, who were evangelized after the resurrection. Notice how the writer feels free to impose the allegorical meaning of gentile on a Jewish reality.

21. The fanciful development is based on the fact that, from the later viewpoint, Jesus is high priest. This allows OT data (cf. Ex 28:33) regarding the high priest to be transferred to him and then given a further allegorical treatment. The interpretation here differs from that of Josephus, who sees the golden bells and pomegranates as symbolizing thunder and lightning, respectively (Josephus, *Jewish War*, V, 231–235). Eucherius explains cymbals as "the lips that confess God" (Euch *Form* p. 57 10). Gregory explains the little bells as the priest's righteous works and the pomegranates as symbolizing the unity of faith (*Reg* p. 192 80–82; *Pastoral Care*, pp. 53–54). Cymbals ring out just as believers must let their faith ring out; the pomegranate contains a great number of seeds, all held in unity.

22. Jerome *Math* p. 59 1374–1377; PetC *Ser* 36.4 p. 210 109–113. The correspondence of the number of years mentioned in the case of each leads to a consideration very similar to that of Paul in Romans, where he compares the situation of both Jews and gentiles and rates both as equally sinful. The only recourse for both is to imitate Abraham, who was made righteous because of his trusting faith (Gen 15:6; cited in Rom 4:3).

CHAPTER 6

Then, coming *to his hometown* (Mark 6:1), Jesus is called *the carpenter's son*.[1] This is to be taken in a mystical sense. The *carpenter* is the one who made *the dawn and the sun*.[2] This refers to the church in its early and later stages. The healing of girl and woman is a figure of these stages.

It continues: **A prophet is not without honor except in his hometown** (Mark 6:4).

Derision often accompanies very lowly origins, as in the case of "What *is the son of Jesse?*"[3] But the Lord regards the lowly *and recognizes the haughty from afar*.[4]

The twelve apostles are then sent out (cf. Mark 6:7). And they were given instructions about how to teach, so that word and deed would accompany each other, and so that visible acts of power would shine forth, along with the in-

---

1. It is the parallel, Matt 13:55, that has the phrase "the carpenter's son."
2. Hil *Matt* 9:6, p. 210. Cf. Ps 74:16, where God is addressed as making dawn and sun. The Gallican version of the Psalter uses the term *fabricatus*, which links up with the term *faber*, i.e., "carpenter," here. Jesus is God's son and therefore the "maker's" son. Dawn and sun are taken as an allegory of the development of the church. Possibly, there is a suggestion of the church having an OT and NT phase because of the earlier meaning proposed for the girl and woman. The healing stories immediately preceding (Mark 5:21–43) are referred to as a parallel development because of the progression from girl to woman.
3. Cf. 1 Sam 25:10, where David, the son of Jesse, is held in contempt.
4. Cf. Ps 138:6.

visible promises.[5] So *they anointed* the sick *with oil* (Mark 6:13); they strengthened their weakness with the power of faith.[6]

Then *Herod heard* the name of Jesus being publicized (cf. Mark 6:14). It is
not possible for *a lamp* to be hidden under a measure.[7]

**When he heard this, Herod said, "I beheaded John and here he has
risen from the dead" (Mark 6:16).**

There is a clear irony in this pronouncement from Herod, the man in skins
of fur.[8] He cuts off the Law's head, which is Christ, from the body to which it
belongs, the Jewish people.[9] It is given to the gentile girl, that is the Roman
church. The girl gives it to her adulterous mother, that is the synagogue, which
will finally come to believe.[10] The body of John is buried, while the head is
placed on a dish. The human letter is covered, while the spirit is honored upon
the altar and is received.[11]

The text goes on: *The apostles* rejoin *Jesus* and report to him what they
did and taught (cf. Mark 6:30). *The rivers return to the place from where they
flow out.*[12] Thanks be to God forever—the apostles offer what they have
received.

5. Cf. Mark 16:20.

6. The symbolic force of anointing with oil is made explicit with the reference to
strengthening.

7. Cf. Mark 4:21.

8. Jerome *Nom* p. 140 17. The Latin *pellicius* appears to suggest an irony to the commentator because of the contrast between the clothing of Herod and that of John the Baptist. The name Herod is explained according to Jerome's glossary. Certainly Herod did not
intend to be ironic.

9. Jerome *Zach* p. 779 60–61. The allegory is very compressed and not immediately
evident. The head of John the Baptist is taken to represent Christ. The body of John represents the Jewish people. The separation of the head from the body is seen as representing
the rejection of Jesus by the Jews. It is possible that the author sees an irony in the fact that
the head of the Law is separated from those who have the Law.

10. C. Arles *Ser* 163 p. 671 no. 643.3. The Law passes over to the care of the gentile
Roman church. The Jews, in due course, receive back the gift of the Law from this church.
The assurance of the eventual coming to Christian faith of the Jews is derived from Rom
11:25–26.

11. The allegory changes. John's separated head and body now represent, respectively,
the spirit and letter of the Bible (or of the Law?). This distinction between Christian and
Jewish exegesis has already been proposed. The mention of the dish appears to lead the
author to think of the communion paten on the altar. This involves the resumption of the
prior coding of John's head as Christ.

12. Eccles 1:7.

And he said to them, "Come aside," etc., as far as **time to eat** (Mark 6:31).

This is found only in Mark. He leads aside those whom he has chosen so that, living among evil people, they will not seek evil; like Lot in Sodom, or Job in the land of Hus, or Obadiah in the house of Ahab.[13] And he said to them, *rest for a while* (Mark 6:31). They are like birds in the branches of the mustard shrub.[14] There is little rest here for the holy ones and long hours of hard work, but later they are told to *rest from their labors*.[15]

For there were many coming and going, and they did not have time to eat (Mark 6:31).

In Noah's Ark the animals inside were trying to get out and those outside were trying to force their way in.[16] It certainly happens like that in the church. Judas withdrew and the thief approached.[17] As long as there is someone falling away from the faith, the church will not rest without sadness. *Rachel, weeping for her children*, refused to be consoled.[18] There is no banquet here where new wine is drunk.[19] When will *a new song* be sung in a new heaven and in a new earth by new people, *when this mortal being will have put on immortality?*[20]

As it continues: Five thousand men will be fed in the evening of life *with five loaves of bread and two fish*, and *twelve baskets* full of fragments are collected, as was done in the eighth miracle (cf. Mark 6:41).[21] This will be when the twelve sit upon thrones, *judging the twelve tribes of Israel*,[22] who are *the frag-*

---

13. A negative assessment of the world is again offered. Parallels are given from the OT: Lot (Gen 13:12–13), Job (Job 1:1), and Obadiah (1 Kings 18:3–19).

14. The mustard shrub (Mark 4:32) was described previously as the resting place for "the poor of Christ."

15. Rev 14:13.

16. Cf. Gen 6:10. There is clearly an allusion to a legendary development of the biblical story here, but I have been unable to identify it.

17. The author gives examples of ongoing apostasy and conversion, seen in the stories of Judas (Mark 14:10–11) and the "good thief" (Luke 23:40–43).

18. The sad story of Rachel (Jer 31:15; Matt 2:17–18) typifies one aspect of the present existence of the church.

19. Cf. Is 25:6–10; Joel 3:8.

20. Cf. Rev 5:9; 21:1; 1 Cor 15:54.

21. The eighth miracle (Mark 6:34–44) is allegorized slightly in this summary to allow an answer to the question just posed.

22. Cf. Matt 19:28 par.

ments of Abraham, Isaac and Jacob.[23] When will *the remnants of Israel be saved?*[24] When we will see *face to face* that which we read written about Christ *in the Law of Moses, the Prophets and the Psalms.*[25]

So, after these things, *at the fourth watch of the night,* Jesus, walking upon the sea, calms the swell and said, *Take courage, it is I* (Mark 6:48). Because *we will see him as he is.*[26] Then the wind and the storm will cease as Jesus sits, that is reigns, in the boat, which is the universal church.

Thus, the text continues: **And all those who touched him were healed** (Mark 6:56).

When *sorrow and groaning will flee away.*[27]

23. The fragments (Mark 6:43) are the descendants of the three patriarchs. Below, in treating of the second multiplication story, the fragments (Mark 8:8) are understood as "the first weeks," while in the interpolated homily (see the appendix) they are seen as standing for the words of the Holy Spirit. These three patriarchs appear to be named as representatives of the worthy members of the Jewish race who will be saved.

24. Rom 9:27.

25. Cf. 1 Cor 13:12; cf. Luke 24:44. The logic of the string of associations is not easy to grasp. The eventual conversion of the Jews is brought up again, gratuitously in the present context.

26. 1 John 3:2. For a moment, the disciples saw him as he is, i.e., in his divine nature.

27. The author comments by quoting Is 35:10 (= 51:11), which he sees as fulfilled by Jesus' ministry.

CHAPTER 7

And the Pharisees gathered around him, etc. (Mark 7:1).

With a two-pronged argument, he counters the excessive ranting of the Pharisees by means of the chiding of Moses and Isaiah,[1] so that we may overcome opposing heresies with the words of Scripture. They saw the disciples eating bread with defiled, that is, unwashed, hands.[2] This signifies the future communion of the gentiles. The cleanliness and the baptism of the Pharisees are useless. The unwashed apostolic community *stretches its branches even as far as the sea*, which is greater than the guilt.[3] However, the tradition of the Pharisees in regard to tables and dishes is not to be maintained, but is to be cut off and eradicated. Often the commandments of God give place to the traditions of men.

After these things, we have the ninth sign (cf. Mark 7:24). The Tyro-Phoenician woman,[4] whose daughter had an unclean spirit, entered and *fell at his feet* (Mark 7:25). She was a *gentile* woman. She petitions on behalf of the daughter who is our mother, the Roman church. The daughter of the possessed stands for a barbaric western nation. Her faith changes a dog into a sheep.[5]

---

1. Referring to Jesus' quoting of Isaiah in Is 29:13 (Mark 7:6–7) and of Moses in Ex 20:12; 21:17 (Mark 7:10).

2. In the Latin, the terms *communibus manibus*, i.e., "unwashed hands," suggest easily *communio* and *communicatio*. The gentiles are not bound to Jewish ritual observance.

3. Ps 80:11; cf. Micah 7:19.

4. See the comment on the other instance of this unusual form in the prologue.

5. Aug *Sym* p. 187 58–59. The mother enables her daughter to meet the Shepherd.

She longs for the crumbs, that is, understanding, not for the unbroken loaf of the letter.[6] The faithful, prudent, and humble woman deserves to get what she demands.[7]

And leaving again the territories of Tyre, he came by way of Sidon, etc. (Mark 7:31).

Mark is the only one to tell us about the tenth miracle at this point. The deaf and dumb man is led in. Tyre stands for "a narrow place."[8] It represents Judea, to which the Lord says, *The bed is narrow, and the blanket is short; it cannot cover both.*[9] As a result he transfers himself to other peoples (cf. Mark 6:53). Sidon means "hunting."[10] It represents our wild and untamed people.[11]

To the sea of Galilee (Mark 7:31).

This means "waves and whirls."[12]

Through the midst of the Decapolis region (Mark 7:31).

Decapolis is interpreted as the "commandments of the Decalogue." By means of the apostles the Savior is brought to save the nations. To *the young man* who asked him what he should do, he replied, *You know the commandments.*[13]

---

6. Scriptural exegesis is imaged as a breaking of the loaf into edible pieces to reach true understanding. This is contrasted with the alleged Jewish keeping to the letter.

7. Both mother and daughter are gentiles, taken to represent gentile churches. In contrast, at Mark 5:28–29, the gentile church was represented by a Jewish woman. Because it had sent out missionaries throughout western Europe, many churches regarded Rome as the mother church. The reference to the "western nation" is tantalizingly vague. It could refer to either the author's native land or his actual residence. This phrase "western nation" forms part of Bischoff's consideration of the work as Irish. He compares it to a phrase in Columbanus's First Letter, where Ireland is described as *occidentales apices* ("Turning-Points," p. 153, n. 42). It may be remarked that Columbanus's phrase is more specific, i.e., "the most westerly point." Greeks and Romans called other peoples "barbaric." Does the use of the term suggest anything about the author?

8. Jerome *Nom* p. 139 27–28.

9. Cf. Is 28:20. The shift from Jew to gentile is harped on by the commentator. The author has a strong consciousness of his identity as a gentile succeeding the Jews.

10. Jerome *Nom* p. 138 9.

11. Hunting takes place in the wilds, and by association he makes a reference to either his native land or his present abode.

12. Jerome *Nom* p. 131 2 (*volubilis*); Euch *Ins* p. 144 22 (*volubiles*).

13. Cf. Matt 19:20, which specifies the man as "young." The Markan parallel (10:17–22) does not have this detail. Jesus' reply is drawn from Luke 18:20. The story is alluded to because of the word "commandments" in both places.

And they bring to him a deaf and dumb man (Mark 7:32).

The human race is consumed by various plagues in its many limbs, as if it were one person. It is summed up in the first man created.[14] He becomes blind while he sees; he becomes deaf when he hears; while he smells he wipes his nose; he loses his speech while he speaks; he is maimed while he stretches out his hand; he is stooped while he is raised up; he has dropsy while he desires;[15] he limps while he is moving; he is covered in leprosy while he is stripped naked; he is filled with a demon while he desired divinity; he dies *the death* while he brazenly makes excuses for having behaved disobediently.[16]

And they beseech him to lay a hand on him (Mark 7:32).

Many righteous people and patriarchs *and prophets* hoped and desired that the Lord would become incarnate.[17]

The Lord, **taking him aside from the crowd** (Mark 7:33).

Whoever deserves to be healed is always led aside from confused thoughts, disordered actions, and undisciplined talk.[18] The fingers inserted in his ears are the words of the Spirit, of whom it is said, *This is the finger of God*, and the heavens are *the works of your fingers*.[19]

14. Greg *Hom* 2 1082 C. The deaf and dumb man is allegorized as the human race. Since all came from the *protoplastus* (the first man formed), all can be said to be contained in one. The human race is presented in a pitiful state, with many ailments which nullify all efforts. Three of the five senses are mentioned, together with the faculty of speech, movements of hand and foot, and the condition of the skin. Similarities with Gregory occur. Gregory is fond of taking a character to represent the entire human race (e.g., *Forty Gospel Homilies*, pp. 42, 95). The passage is reminiscent of, though not exactly parallel with, a passage in Gregory's *Pastoral Care* (pp.40–44), where he comments on Lev 21:17–20. That desire or concupiscence is affected by dropsy appears to reflect the medical science of the period. Gregory associates a similar medical condition with inclinations to lechery (*Pastoral Care*, p. 44).

15. C. Arles *Ser* 223 p. 881; Greg *Reg* p. 170 83–106.

16. The scene in the Garden of Eden is recalled. The serpent assured Eve that they would not die the death (Gen 3:4). They wrongly aspired to divine status. The section closes as it opens, with a mention of the first human beings.

17. Cf. Matt 13:17. The Incarnation of the Lord is imaged as God touching humanity represented by the man.

18. The story of the healing is transformed into a lesson in spirituality, stressing the importance of silence and recollection.

19. Ex 8:19; cf. Ps 8:4a. The Holy Spirit is described as "the finger of the Father's right hand" in "Veni, Creator Spiritus," a hymn to be attributed probably to Rabanus Maurus (776–856), abbot of Fulda.

And spitting, he touched his tongue (Mark 7:33).

The spit from the flesh of the Lord is divine wisdom,[20] which loosens the bond of the lips of the human race so that it can recite, "I believe in God, the Father almighty, etc."[21]

And looking up to heaven, he groaned (Mark 7:34).

That is, he teaches us both to sigh,[22] and to elevate to heaven the treasure of our heart.[23] It is through a sigh of heartfelt compunction that the frivolous joy of the flesh is purged, as it is said, *I roared from the groaning of my heart.*[24]

And he said to him, "Effeta," which means "Be opened" (Mark 7:34).

One believes with the heart to be justified, one confesses with the mouth to be saved.[25]

And at once his ears were opened, and the bond on his tongue was loosened, and he spoke properly (Mark 7:35).

The ears were opened for hymns, canticles, and psalms.[26] He loosens the tongue so that it may utter the good news,[27] which neither floggings nor threats can restrain. As Paul says, *I am fettered,* but *the word of God* in me *is not tied up.*[28]

And he ordered them to tell no one (Mark 7:36).

He taught that one must not glory in acts of power, but in the cross and in humiliation.

20. Greg *Ez* I 10 p. 154 351–352.
21. A similar use of spittle formed part of the traditional rite of Baptism. Gregory explains the spittle as indicative of wisdom in speaking of God. The author's development of this is his own. It seems that he was content to take the occasional idea and image from Gregory and adapt them.
22. Greg *Ez* I 10 p. 153 248–350.
23. Cf. Mark 10:21 par.; cf. Matt 6:20–21.
24. Ps 38:8b.
25. As he often does, the author offers a comment by quoting another text of Scripture (Rom 10:10). Jesus restores speech to the man, symbolizing the supernatural efficacy of the rite of Baptism, enabling Christians to proclaim their faith.
26. Cf. Eph 5:19.
27. Cf. Ps 45:1.
28. Cf. Eph 3:1; 2 Tim 2:9.

The more he ordered them, the more they broadcast it (Mark 7:36).

A city situated on a hill, conspicuous like Rubia, cannot be hidden.[29] Humility always comes before glory.[30]

29. Cf. Matt 5:14. The reference to Rubia is found in only one manuscript (Angers 275), but this is a very important one, the only manuscript to preserve the original unexpanded version of the commentary. Unfortunately, my efforts to determine this location have proved unsuccessful to date. There would appear to be an important clue to provenance here.

30. The prohibition of Christ has been a problem for commentators throughout the centuries, involving discussion of the so-called messianic secret. This commentator deals with the issue by linking it with the pattern of Christ's life, involving suffering and death, and offered as an example for all.

CHAPTER 8

⁕

By means of the eleventh miracle seven loaves of bread are broken for 4,000 hungry people (cf. Mark 8:5); a few little fish are blessed; and seven basketfuls of scraps are collected. The seven loaves stand for the seven gifts of the Holy Spirit. The 4,000 represents the New Testament year with its four seasons; the seven baskets are the first seven churches. The scraps of bread, understood mystically, represent the first week.[1] The little blessed fish are the books of the New Testament, since the risen Lord demands *a piece of roast fish.*[2] He also offers *fish placed on* burning coals to the disciples on the occasion of the catch of fish.[3]

---

1. Cf. Gen 1:1–2:4.
2. Cf. Luke 24:41–42.
3. Cf. John 21:9. The earlier feeding of the multitude (Mark 6:32–44) was only briefly noted. This one is allegorized in detail. In the homily (appendix), the scraps collected in the seven baskets are understood as the words of the Spirit, while the baskets are the seven churches. The four in the 4,000 is taken as the four seasons. One scholar has suggested that liturgical seasons are meant, presumably Advent, Lent, Eastertide, and Ordinary Time (G. Morin, "Un commentaire romain," p. 359). The seven churches are the seven churches to get letters from Paul or possibly the seven churches of the book of Revelation. The first week is the week of creation in Gen 1. An unusual feature occurs when the author explains the basis of his interpretation of the fish by pointing to the association of the risen Lord with fish (cf. Luke 24:34–35; cf. John 21:9).

Afterward, **they come to Bethsaida** (Mark 8:22).

Bethsaida is explained as the "house of the valley,"[4] and what does it refer to, if not this world which is *a valley of tears*?[5] For the twelfth miracle, *they lead forward* a blind man who does not see either in front or behind, that is to say, what was, what is, and what will be.[6] And they ask *him to touch him*. Who is the one touched if not the one who feels remorse?[7] And he takes *the hand of the blind man* (Mark 8:23), in order that he may lament over the blindness of his heart, and just like Jeremiah over the fall of the city of God,[8] weep copiously over his soul. He leads him *outside of the town*, that is to say, outside of the vicinity of evils. For *bad conversations corrupt good morals*.[9]

And spitting in his eyes (Mark 8:23).

That he might see the will of God through the breath of the Holy Spirit.[10] *Laying hands on him*, he asks him *if he saw anything*. Through the works of the Lord, he sees His majesty. The creator is recognized from the greatness of the creature.[11]

And looking, he said, "I see men walking as if they were trees" (Mark 8:24).

That is to say, he considered all men superior to himself, and, like David, judged himself unworthy to be called a man but "a dead dog" and "a flea."[12] Again, Jesus placed his hands *upon his eyes* so that he might see *everything clearly*, that is, through visible works he might understand invisible things which the eye has not seen. And with the eye of a clean heart, he might behold clearly

---

4. Jerome *Nom* p. 91 27; p. 135 21–22.

5. Cf. Ps 84:6 (var.).

6. The story is made more explicit by adding the details "in front and behind," and then these details are given an allegorical sense.

7. Physical touch is given a moral sense. The spiritual state of the blind man is given priority by the author, although there is no suggestion of this in the text.

8. Cf. the book of Lamentations attributed to Jeremiah.

9. Again, the literal sense is given a moral application, buttressed by the use of 1 Cor 15:33. The translation here follows the Latin Vulgate and is a good example of where the biblical text used by the author differs from the one we use today.

10. The spitting action of Jesus is described as the breath of the Spirit. This is probably because of the expulsion of breath involved in spitting. Previously, Jesus' spit is construed as divine wisdom.

11. Cf. Wis 13:5. The author never misses an opportunity to teach and remind his readers of basic principles.

12. The man's words are construed in the terms of 1 Sam 24:14.

the state of his soul after the blight of sin. For *blessed are the clean of heart because they will see God.*[13]

And he sent him **to his house** (Mark 8:26).

So that he could see in himself what he did not see before. For a man despairing of his salvation does not think he can, in any way, do the very thing he can easily accomplish when he is enlightened by hope.[14]

And he says to him, **If you go into the village tell no one** (Mark 8:26).

In other words, "tell the neighbors continually about your blindness and not about this miracle." As Paul says, *I was a blasphemer,* etc., because I persecuted *the church of God.*[15]

After that **he began to teach them** that **the Son of Man had to suffer much** and rise on the third day (cf. Mark 8:31).

Like an experienced helmsman, who taking precautions in good weather against a storm, wishes his sailors to be prepared.[16]

For this reason he says, **"If anyone wishes to come after me, let him deny himself"** (Mark 8:34).

That is to say, one thing brings about the other. After the verification of the cross, the glory of the resurrection is displayed.

13. Matt 5:8.
14. This appears to take the physical act of "going home" as representing a journey inward to find his true self and potential. Physical sight stands for insight.
15. The admonition of Christ is developed in order to imply a spiritual lesson. He cites the example of Paul, who acknowledged his sinful former way of life (1 Tim 1:13 combined with Phil 3:6).
16. Forewarned is forearmed, the author remarks, and illustrates this with a nautical example. Can anything about the author's identity be deduced from this? Does such an example spring from his own immediate experience? Other nautical examples can be recalled: The "currach" type of boat is specified (at Mark 1:19 and at Mark 4:38); he mentions sea merchants (on Mark 1:15); he compares the cross to the mast of a ship (at Mark 15:21).

CHAPTER 9

❦

And so it continues with the thirteenth miracle.

After six days he was *transfigured* on a high mountain in the presence of his disciples (cf. Mark 9:1), so that they would not fear the scandals of the cross, since they had seen with their own eyes the glory of the future resurrection.

And they kept the matter to themselves, discussing what it should mean—"when he shall be risen from the dead" (Mark 9:9).

Mark is the only one to give this. When *death* will have been swallowed up *in victory,*[1] *the former things will be forgotten, and will not come to mind;*[2] when *the Lord* will take away *the filth* of the daughter of Sion,[3] wiping away *every tear from all the faces* of the saints.[4]

---

1. Cf. 1 Cor 15:54.
2. Is 65:17; Cf. Luke 24:38.
3. Cf. Is 4:4.
4. Cf. Is 25:8; Rev 7:17; 21:4. He suggests a meaning for this text, proper to Mark, by listing other texts of an eschatological type, expressing final triumph, and lasting joy and happiness.

And coming to his disciples, he saw a big crowd around them, and the scribes arguing with them (Mark 9:13).

Man has no rest *under the sun*.[5] Envy always kills the little ones,[6] while great lightnings strike the mountains.[7] Some speaking with faith, others seeing by good fortune, come together to the church.[8]

Seeing him, the people were amazed and frightened (Mark 9:14).

There is no fear in love.[9] Fear is characteristic of slaves; amazement of fools.[10]

And he asked them, "What are you discussing among you?" (Mark 9:15).

The Lord knows what he asks, so that confession may produce salvation, and so that the grumbling of our heart be eased by devout words such as, *Declare your iniquities beforehand, that you may be justified*.[11]

Afterward, we have the fourteenth miracle. *One of the crowd* brings forward the son with the unclean spirit, etc.[12] The Savior cured the one whom the disciples were not able to cure. The lack of faith of both was an obstacle to the healing. The spirit torments him, foaming at the mouth, grinding his teeth and he becomes weak. The sinner foams at the mouth with foolishness; he grinds its teeth with anger; he becomes weak from sloth. The spirit torments him as he approaches salvation. Who is his food? The chosen ones, whom he wants to draw into his belly through terrors and injuries, as in the case of Job.[13] Jesus

5. Eccles 1:3.
6. Cf. Job 5:2b.
7. Cf. Horace, *Odes* 2.10 10–12. The author is fond of aiming his commentary at those in authority. Men in high and low station are subject to trials. Unimportant folk envy the prominent, but they are in danger also. Important people such as the apostles (and their successors) can expect controversy.
8. The crowd that gathers is made of diverse elements, not all there for the same reason, and this is taken as pointing to the makeup of the church.
9. Cf. 1 John 4:18.
10. The reactions of the people are judged inappropriate.
11. Is 43:26 (Old Latin version).
12. The comments do not follow the sequence of the narrative. He anticipates the later explanation by Jesus of the failure of the disciples. The reason given, lack of faith, is stressed more in the synoptic parallels (Matt 17:20 par.), than in Mark, where prayer and fasting are posited (9:29).
13. Greg *Hom* 25 1194 C–1195 A; *Iob* 33 vii pp. 1684–1685 (on Job 40:19). There is here what might be termed a "ghost allusion" to a homily of Gregory, in which he imagines Satan seizing Christ's flesh as food. The echo of this is puzzling unless the original is recognized. Gregory uses the imagery of Job 41 to portray God as a fisherman using the body of Christ as the visible bait on the invisible hook of Christ's divinity. The devil craves

asks about the duration, and the father says, *from infancy*. Here is signified the gentile people, among which the useless cult of idols developed, so that they foolishly sacrificed their children to demons.[14]

So it continues: **And frequently** he throws **him into the fire and into water** (cf. Mark 9:21).

For some gentiles worship fire, others water.[15]

And Jesus says to him, **If you can believe** (Mark 9:22).

This points to the fact of free will.[16]

All things are possible to the one who believes (Mark 9:22).

What are *all things* if not those which are sought, in the name of Jesus, which means "salvation"?

The father of the boy said, with tears, **I believe, help my unbelief** (cf. Mark 9:23).

Our belief is weak, like curved planks,[17] unless it exists joined to the strength of the help of God. Faith combined with tears gets what is prayed for, as is shown in the words, *Let it be done to you according to your faith.*[18]

---

to devour the flesh as food and then is exposed to deadly attack (*Forty Gospel Homilies*, pp. 196–197). The phrasing is different but the basic imagery is the same. Cf. Job 6:4, which serves as a paradigm for demonic possession.

14. For some reason the author thought of the gentiles and uses an incidental detail of the story as an allegory to condemn their long-standing idolatry. His mention of child sacrifice may be a reference to biblical data (e.g., 2 Kings 3:27) or perhaps to the experience of the writer in Europe.

15. The reference to worshiping of water suits the Celtic areas of western Europe where the holy wells testify to missionaries' attempts to baptize pagan customs. Pagan holy wells were commonplace in Gaul and in Ireland. In the seventh century Tírechán wrote of St. Patrick's frequent encounters with druids at wells (L. Bieler and F. Kelly, eds., *Patrician Texts in the Book of Armagh*, pp. 152–155). "It has been estimated that there are over 6000 springs in France which were venerated in pre-Christian times" (J. N. Hillgarth, "Modes of Evangelization of Western Europe in the Seventh Century," p. 327).

16. There is a shift in the allegorical treatment of the narrative. Is this a reflection of theological analysis of the role of the will in faith? Later (at Mark 11:2 and 12:1), the author draws attention again to free will. For a fuller consideration of the free will issue, see the footnote at Mark 11:2.

17. The Latin is difficult; the manuscripts vary. I read *rostrata ligna*, which could also be translated, perhaps, as "bent trees."

18. Cf. Matt 9:29.

And when Jesus saw a crowd rushing (Mark 9:24).

Mark is the only one to give us what follows.[19]

He rebuked the unclean spirit (Mark 9:24).

The Lord's threat is his power.

Deaf and dumb spirit (Mark 9:24).

They attribute to the spirit the evil that it is exhibiting in the man, while this spirit never hears nor speaks what a repentant sinner hears and speaks.[20]

Go out of him and do not enter him again (Mark 9:24).

He goes out of the man, and never returns if the key of humble love secures his heart, and the man controls the door of the fort. For this reason the prophet says, *Be for me a protecting God and a fortress, that you may make me safe.*[21]

And he became like **one dead** (Mark 9:25).

Those who are healed are told, *You are dead, and your life is hidden with Christ in God.*[22] For this reason, the sickness of Christians is not death, but only the likeness of death.

When they had gone into the house, his disciples **ask him** why they were not able to cast him out, since he had given them the power of casting out demons (cf. Mark 9:27).

And he said to them, this kind is cast out **only by prayer and fasting** (Mark 9:28).

Foolishness has to do with fleshly indulgence, and is healed by fasting and prayer; anger and sloth are driven out through prayer. The proper medicine must be used for each wound. What is used for the heel does not cure the eye.[23] The passions of the body must be healed by fasting, and the afflictions of the mind must be healed by prayer.

---

19. Mark, unlike the other Gospels, gives a detailed account of the exorcism.
20. Aug *Civ* 8:19 p. 236 45–46.
21. Ps 31:2b. The psalmist is regularly referred to as a prophet.
22. Col 3:3.
23. The point here has a loose association with Paul's reflections in 1 Cor 12:21–22.

And they came to Capernaum (Mark 9:32).

Capernaum means the "town of consolation."[24] This interpretation follows appropriately the preceding statement which runs: *he was killed, on the third day he will rise* (Mark 9:31). *The grain of wheat* dies so that many times as much may be gathered. If it does not die, *it remains alone.*[25]

When they were in the house, he asked them, "What were you discussing along the way?" (Mark 9:32).

For along the way they were discussing leadership. The locale suited the discussion. For as leadership begins, so it is given up, and all the while it is held, it is slipping away. Also there is no certainty as to which lodging place, that is which day, it may finish up.[26] Therefore he says, "Who wishes to be first *like the child,* let him be *the servant*" (cf. Mark 9:34–35).

It is better for you to enter into life maimed, that is to say, without leadership ambitions, than to go **into inextinguishable fire with two hands** (Mark 9:42).

The *two hands* stand for leadership and pride. Cut off pride and maintain a humble rule.[27]

The **worm does not die, and the fire is not extinguished** (Mark 9:43).[28]

The worm is the realization that comes too late, and the fire is unending punishment. For this reason, the prophet says, *Walk in the light of your fire and in the flames which you have kindled for yourselves.*[29]

24. Jerome *Nom* p. 139 11–12.
25. Cf. John 12:24.
26. The author spins an allegory for all leaders out of an analysis of the nature of a journey. The disciples were moving along, signifying the transitory aspect of all human power and authority. No matter how absolute or secure this power seems, it is actually decreasing every day. Every journey has an built-in uncertainty about time of arrival because of unforeseen delays.
27. The verse is interpreted in regard to the previous discussion of leadership. The linking of leadership and pride maintains the cautionary tone adopted in respect of the leadership role.
28. The manuscripts read "the worm," not "their worm."
29. Is 50:11b. It is important to note that this text from Isaiah, in its original setting, does not speak about the fires of hell. The commentator is working with an understanding of Scripture which allows him to see allusions in texts whose wording is open to such a literal meaning when removed from context. This is to be distinguished from a later approach to the Bible, known as the *sensus plenior,* which would see texts susceptible of a fuller meaning in the light of later revelation.

Everything will be salted with fire (Mark 9:48).

And every victim is salted. The Lord's victim is the human race.[30] In this life it is salted by means of wisdom so that in the next life[31] the blood, which is a prison of rottenness and a mother of worms,[32] may be consumed and tested by purifying fire.[33]

Salt is good, etc. (Mark 9:49).

The insipid salt stands for the person who loves being a leader.[34] Such persons do not dare to rebuke nor to proclaim their faith, lest they be ejected from the synagogue.[35] Such people love *human glory more than* the glory of God.[36]

Have salt in yourselves and have peace among you (Mark 9:49).

Let love of neighbor soothe the salty tang of correction. Let the salt of justice preserve the love of neighbor.[37]

---

30. Consideration of the human race as whole is a feature of the author's concerns.

31. "This life/next life" translates the Latin *hic/illic* (literally, "here/there").

32. Salt was a standard way of preserving such things as meat or fish, by preventing worms.

33. Some scholars see a reference to purgatory here (*purgatorio igne*), but it could simply refer to fire in the senses already proposed (Wohlenberg, "Ein vergessener," p. 466; Morin, "Un commentaire romain," p. 358). The phrase is altogether typical of the early Middle Ages, as other texts of the seventh century testify. Historians of purgatory stress that we must be sensitive to a development and that we are still in the early stages in the case of texts like the present. See Jacques Le Goff, *The Birth of Purgatory,* pp. 96–103; also appendix 2, "*Purgatorium:* The History of a Word," pp. 362–366. Brian Grogan concluded that the "early Irish Church was familiar with the concept of purgatory as distinct from hell" ("Eschatological Teaching in the Early Irish Church," p. 50).

34. Though the "insipid" part of Mark 9:49 is not explicitly quoted, the author presumes knowledge of it, as he uses it, once again, to deliver a critique of those with leadership aspirations. Reluctance to correct others was condemned at Mark 1:3.

35. Cf. John 9:22.

36. Cf. John 12:43.

37. The words of Jesus are themselves in the metaphorical mode and lend themselves readily to expansion along this line.

CHAPTER 10

When they were in the house the disciples questioned him again about
the same matter (Mark 10:10).

This is proper to Mark. Repetition of knowledge of a term shows not fas-
tidiousness but a hunger and thirst. As Wisdom declares, *Those who eat me* are
hungry again, *and those who drink of me* are thirsty again.[1] The mellifluous sayings of wisdom, when savored with some care, yield a variegated flavor. When
the Lord rains down manna to be eaten, it became soft as wax in the sun,[2] and
resulted in softened sayings such as *the righteous will shine like the sun in the kingdom of their Father.*[3] The manna is hardened over the fire,[4] like *bread*, strengthening *the heart of man*,[5] for harsh sayings such as, *If anyone wants to come after me,
let him deny himself, and take up his cross and follow me.*[6]

The Pharisees questioned him as to whether it is permissible for a
man to divorce his wife. They were testing him (Mark 10:2).

Soon after we read: *When they were in the house his disciples questioned him
again about the same thing* (Mark 10:10), that is to say, about the married state,
as in the next section.[7]

1. Sir 24:29.
2. Cf. Ex 16:14–15 and Ex 16:21.
3. Matt 13:43.
4. Cf. Num 11:8.
5. Cf. Ps 104:15.
6. Matt 16:24.
7. The author refers to the first and second questionings, which sandwich the section
dealing with the debate of Jesus with the Pharisees concerning the texts on marriage. This

And he says to them, Whoever divorces a wife, etc. (Mark 10:11).

But what Mark says is: *His disciples questioned him again* (Mark 10:10). It was not the disciples who questioned him previously but the Pharisees; but the second interrogation was by others, that is by the apostles. *Again* refers to the same thing about which the Pharisees asked.

After these things, they came to Jericho.[8] Jericho is interpreted as "moon" or "anathema."[9] The name of the city corresponds to the upcoming suffering of the Lord. The eclipse of the flesh of Christ—Maranatha—is the new moon of the heavenly Jerusalem.[10] And so, leaving Jericho, they approach Jerusalem, that is to say "the vision of peace."[11]

And setting out from Jericho, etc., as far as **he followed him along the road** (Mark 10:46–52).[12]
Bartimaeus, son of Timaeus, a blind man, was sitting by the roadside, begging (Mark 10:46).

The blind man is enlightened by the fifteenth miracle. The blindness, which has occurred partly among the Jews, is illuminated at the end, when he will send Elijah the prophet to them.

Begging by the roadside (Mark 10:46).

Whoever preserves Scripture, while not fulfilling it, is like someone who is hungry and begs while at the table.[13] When he hears that Jesus of Nazareth is passing, he calls out, *Son of David, take pity on me.* The Jewish people is en-

---

"next section" he refers to is section 105 of the Eusebian Canons, mentioned in the prologue. As the following paragraph makes clear, the commentator was preoccupied with what he perceived as an inconsistency in the Markan narrative.

8. Mark 10:13–45 is passed over, and he does not attend to Mark 10:24, 30, 32, all proper to Mark.

9. Jerome *Nom* p. 137 2; p. 157 6.

10. The author sees the death of Jesus both as a curse and as the low point of glory. The new moon occurs in total darkness. Eucherius explains "neomenia" as new moon (*Ins* p. 155 2). "Anathema" or "curse" is linked with the crucifixion by Paul in Gal 3:13 (= Deut 21:23), and this may have inspired the present association. The term "Maranatha," interjected as an exclamation of hope, is similarly found in other texts of the period.

11. Jerome *Nom* p. 146 16.

12. The extent of the pericope is identified, and then the first part to be commented upon (the "lemma") is quoted, Mark 10:46.

13. The Jews are credited with preserving Scripture. Eucherius explains that "table" symbolizes "spiritual nourishment" (*Form* p. 45 17).

lightened through the merits of the Patriarchs. The Lord is *merciful* and *compassionate* to the Jews.[14] He enlightens *the blind*; raises up *those who are cast down*; loves the poor; takes care of *aliens*.[15]

And many rebuke **him so that he may be quiet** (cf. Mark 10:48).

Sins and demons suppress the cry of the poor man, which the Lord heard.[16]

But he cried out the more (Mark 10:48).

When war threatens, hands are to be raised up with a cry to *the rock of help*, namely Jesus of Nazareth.[17]

And he ordered him to be called, and they say to him, **"Take courage, get up, he is calling you"** (Mark 10:49).

How harmonious is the pattern of salvation! First we hear, then we cry out, afterward we are called, finally we rise up. We hear through the prophets, we call through faith, we are called through the apostles, we rise through repentance, we are stripped bare through baptism, we enquire through our will.[18]

And so it continues: **He threw aside his cloak, jumped up and came** (Mark 10:50).

He is said to jump nude out of *the old man*,[19] just like the stag bounding upon the mountains, jumping on the hills.[20] Laying aside sluggishness, gazing on the patriarchs, prophets and apostles on high, he reaches out to the things above.[21]

14. Cf. James 5:11.

15. Cf. Ps 145:8. Just as the Psalm first referred to OT Jews, now Jesus cares for the blind man, a symbol for the Jewish people in NT times.

16. Cf. Ps 9:12b. The bystanders are allegorized as trying to prevent the cry of the poor from reaching God. The allusion to the Psalm text broadens the application in reassuring us that God will always hear us.

17. Cf. 1 Sam 7:12b. The gratuitous reference to war suggests perhaps that this was on the mind of the author. Apart from topicality, it is not possible to suggest anything more precise in regard to dating and location of the commentary.

18. The pattern of the details of the story are allegorized cleverly to sketch out the sequence of events in a typical Christian conversion. This allows the commentator to see an overall harmony in the salvific actions of God. There is basic "ascetical theology" or spirituality being taught here. The Gospel text provides a pedagogic aid.

19. Cf. Eph 4:22; cf. Col 3:9; Jerome *Ep* 125.20 p. 142.

20. Cf. Song 2:8–9.

21. Cf. Col 3:2.

Jesus said to him, "What do you want me to do for you?" (Mark 10:51).

Jesus notes his eager will, and rewards him by fulfilling his desire. For this reason he says elsewhere, Anything *you ask for in prayer, believing, you will receive.*[22]

The blind man said to him, "Rabbi,[23] **that I may see"** (Mark 10:51).

He asks one thing *from the Lord.* This is what he wants, that he see *the will of the Lord,* and then, seeing, that he visit *his temple.*[24]

And so the text continues, **Jesus, however,** said **to him, "Your faith has saved you," and at once he saw and followed him along the way,** next to which he used to beg, and which says: *I am the way, the truth and the life.*[25] This is the narrow way which leads to the high places of Jerusalem and of Bethany, to the Mount of Olives, which is the mountain of light and of consolation.[26]

---

22. Cf. Matt 21:22.

23. The form *Rabbi* is the Latin text; *Rabboni* is the more common reading in the Latin Vulgate tradition.

24. This is an ingenious paraphrase of Ps 27:4, which is accommodated to the situation of the blind man.

25. Greg *Hom* 2 1083 A. There is here a clever play on the term *via*, meaning "road" or "way." Jesus is the way (cf. John 14:6). Gregory the Great, in a homily on the Lukan parallel (Luke 18:31–44), has a very similar development (Gregory the Great, *Forty Gospel Homilies*, p. 95).

26. Rup *Lib* p. 157 502–504. Throughout the treatment of the healing story, the motif of the high places recurs. The details of the physical geography of the holy places mentioned are accurate. If the explanation of the Mount of Olives is meant to be an etymological one, it does not at all correspond to that of Jerome.

CHAPTER 11

And when they drew near to Jerusalem, etc., as far as **Hosanna in the highest** (Mark 11:1–10).

He sent **two of his disciples** (cf. Mark 11:1).

The disciples of Christ are called in pairs and are sent in pairs, because love does not exist when there is a lone person. As it is said, *Woe to the one who is alone*, etc.[1] Two people lead the Hebrews out of Egypt;[2] two carry out the bunch of grapes from the Holy Land[3]: that leaders may combine knowledge and effort. And they make known two commandments from the two tablets;[4] and from two springs they are washed and wash;[5] and they carry the ark of God on two poles;[6] and they will recognize God between two cherubs,[7] singing praise *in mind* and *in spirit*.[8]

---

1. Eccles 4:10.
2. Cf. Ex 6:13.
3. Cf. Num 13:23.
4. Cf. Ex 31:18.
5. Cf, Ex 17:6; cf. Num 20:11.
6. Cf. Ex 25:13–14.
7. Cf. Ex 26:22.
8. Cf. 1 Cor 14:15. Greg *Hom* 17 1139 A. The fact that two disciples are specified in Mark 11:1 is rationalized in terms of Christian love in a manner close to that of Gregory the Great (*Forty Gospel Homilies*, p. 135). This leads to a series of biblical examples and lessons, all involving the number two. None of this development is intrinsically connected to the sense of the Gospel text, and none of the allusions have any connection with each other, apart from the fact that they are all taken from the exodus narrative in Exodus-Numbers.

They bring *a tethered* and unbroken *colt*, which they untie and tame (cf. Mark 11:4). This stands for the gentile people, who stand *in front of the door* of faith, bound by the ropes of their sins. They stand *at a crossroads*, hesitating in free will between life and death.[9] Some asked, *What are you doing?* It is as if they said, *Who can forgive sins?*[10] And they lay their clothes, that is the "best robe" of immortality acquired through the mysteries of baptism.[11]

And Jesus **sat on it** (Mark 11:7).

That is, he began to reign on it.[12] This was *so that sin would not reign* in lascivious flesh,[13] *but righteousness, peace, and joy in the Holy Spirit.*[14] Many laid their clothes on the road beneath the feet of the ass's colt. Whom do the feet represent if not those who carry things for others, and those least important folk

---

It suffices that the number two is used. While the ancient commentator was disposed to see a significance in such incidental details, there is undoubtedly a pedagogic device operating also. Such linking helped people to remember the material of the Bible in detail and helped to drive home religious truths. The lessons are explicitly directed at leaders. It is possible that each example alludes to a particular ministry of these leaders, namely, preaching, baptizing, effecting the presence of Christ at the Eucharist, and chanting the divine praises.

9. Euch *Form* p. 27 7. This simple action becomes an allegorical presentation of the conversion of the gentiles by the missionaries of Christ. Some elements of the allegory are found in Origen (*Commentary on the Gospel according to John*, p. 298). Eucherius explains that an ass stands for "the gentile people." The commentator emphasizes free will. Three times in the commentary, attention is drawn to the issue of free will (at Mark 9:22, here, and at Mark 12:1). In each case it is a gratuitous assertion by the author in the sense that the Gospel text itself does not allude to free will. The raising of the issue indicates that a position is being asserted, and this I would characterize as "semi-Pelagianism." This is a most unfortunate term and an anachronistic one at that, but it serves a purpose, insofar as it does identify a reaction to the extreme Augustinian position, which was itself a reaction to Pelagius, who affirmed the freedom of the will. The author feels the need to teach the fact of free will. In his 1978 article, "Pelagius, Pelagianism and the Early Christian Irish," Joseph F. Kelly briefly examines the interpretation of Mark 11:2 offered by the present commentary, which he regards as "definitely Irish and of the seventh century" (p. 105). He translates: "wavering in the freedom of the will between life and death" (p. 105). This, he writes, "suggests an anti-Pelagian framework," while he concedes "it is precious little to build upon" (pp. 105–106). However, when the present text is taken in conjunction with the two other references, it seems less clear that the author is anti-Pelagian.

10. The loosing calls to mind the loosing from sins. Cf. Mark 2:7.

11. Cf. Luke 15:22. Euch *Form* p. 38 16–17; PetC *Ser* 5.6 p. 40 103–104 (English trans: *Selected Sermons* 17 p. 49.) The clothes are taken as baptismal robes, which were white, symbolizing hope of immortal life. I translate *sacramenta* (plural) as mysteries. Eucherius takes *stola* ("robe") to stand for the garment of Baptism.

12. Every time Jesus sits, the author explains it as reigning, like a king sitting on a throne.

13. Cf. Rom 6:12.

14. Rom 14:17.

whom the apostle appointed to act as judges? While they are not the summit where the Lord sits, nevertheless the directives John gave the soldiers apply to them also.[15]

And others cut branches from trees and spread them on the road (Mark 11:8).

This has more to do with adornment and symbolism than with necessity.[16] The righteous people will flourish *like a palm tree.*[17] They are narrow at the roots but broad in the flowers and the fruits. They are *the good aroma of Christ.*[18] They strew the road with the good reputation of the commandments of God. Those who went in front are the prophets, and those who were following are the apostles, just as *deep calls to deep*, as one Law calls upon the other.[19] They cry out, *Hosanna*, which means "save,"[20] *in the highest* (Mark 11:10), and in the lowest, so that the righteous may build upon the ruin of the angels;[21] and so that those on earth and those under the earth may be set free by the blessed and victorious one,[22] coming *in the name of the Lord* (Mark 11:9), that is, of his father, because "son" has taken the name from "father," and "father" from "son."[23]

And he entered Jerusalem, etc., as far as a **den of thieves** (Mark 11:11–17).

Jesus entered into the Temple, and in the evening he left for Bethany with the Twelve (cf. Mark 11:11). He came to Judea in the morning, but he visits us

15. The feet, the lowest part of the body, represent those at the bottom of the social scale in popular opinion. Some of them are chosen to be judges, according to 1 Cor 6:2–4. While these judges are not as important as Jesus, they have authority and they must not oppress others, as John the Baptist instructed the soldiers in Luke 3:10–14. The author never misses an opportunity to admonish those in authority.

16. I translate *sacramentum* here as "symbolism."

17. Cf. Ps 92:12.

18. The identification of the branches as palm comes from John 12:13. This allows the use of Ps 92:12a. The aptness of the imagery is not total. How are the righteous "narrow"? The contrast of roots and fruit recurs in the commentary. The image changes to one of smell (cf. 2 Cor 2:15).

19. The prophets are understood as those who foretold the one who was to come. Two groups calling out remind the author of Ps 43:7, but the link is merely verbal. The prophets stand for the OT and the apostles for the NT.

20. Euch *Ins* p. 145 19.

21. There appears to be an allusion here, but I am unable to trace it. There is a much later parallel in the anonymous *Liber Quare* (p.109).

22. Cf. Rev 5:13; cf. Phil 2:10; cf. 1 Pet 4:6; cf. John 16:33.

23. "Highest" triggers off its opposite, "lowest." These appear to call to mind, respectively, angels on high in heaven and humans below on earth. The issue of father-son depends on the usage in the parallel text of Matt 21:9, where Jesus is addressed as "Son of David." The remark may betray a sensitivity, due to the Arian controversy, concerning the status of Jesus as "son."

in the evening of the world.[24] The Lord hungers for the salvation of mankind. He sees a fig tree in the distance, covered with leaves but without fruit (cf. Mark 11:13). This stands for the synagogue, clothed in human commandments, and which needs to be swept free of superstitions. He refuses to grant it fruit ever.

Then he entered the Temple, ejected the buyers and sellers, and upset the tables and chairs (cf. Mark 11:15). This refers to those who sell honors and buy positions.[25] For it is written according to Isaiah, *My house will be called a house of prayer.*[26] You, however, have made it *a den of thieves*, according to Jeremiah.[27]

And when it was evening, etc. (Mark 11:19).

This is found only in Mark.[28] He leaves darkness behind him, like the sun from hostile hearts. *He went out from the city* to another which is "benevolent" and "obedient."[29] Returning in the morning, they saw *the fig tree dried up* (Mark 11:20). The sun goes down, the sun rises.[30] The Law is taken away from the scribes and shines out in the apostles. The fig tree, dry from the roots up, is the synagogue from the time of Cain and of the others who must account for all the blood shed from Abel to Zechariah.[31]

Peter said, **"Look, the fig tree that you cursed has withered"** (Mark 11:21).

Peter recognizes it as the dried-up and cut-off root which will be succeeded by the *beautiful fruit-bearing* olive tree, called by the Lord.[32]

---

24. Greg *Hom* 1 1080 C; 4 1090 B; Origen *Ex* 7 p. 230. The author fails to notice that this is proper to Mark. The text is allegorized in terms of a theology of history. The sense of living at the end of time is characteristic of writers around A.D. 600, such as Gregory the Great, who were witnessing the breakup of the Roman Empire (Gregory the Great, *Forty Gospel Homilies*, pp. 10, 122, 124–125).

25. Aug *Ioh* pp. 103 1–104 24; Greg *Hom* 4 1091 C–D; 1092 A; 17 1145 B–C; 39 1295 A.

26. Is 56:7.

27. Cf. Jer 7:11. The buying and selling is read as referring to the abuse of simony. This interpretation is found in Gregory and became standard in later medieval commentaries (Gregory the Great, *Forty Gospel Homilies*, pp. 123, 143–144, 359). The two Scripture passages in Mark, Is 56:7 and Jer 7:11, are identified by the name of the books only.

28. The author calls attention to a detail found only in Mark, but nowhere does he refer to the overall distinctive arrangement of the stories by Mark. The lateness of the day and the dryness of the tree are combined to express the transition from OT to NT. Bethany means "house of obedience," and this underlies the comment of the author.

29. Cf. Mark 11:11–12. Jerome *Nom* p. 135 26–27.

30. Cf. Eccles 1:5.

31. Cf. Gen 4:8; cf. Luke 11:51.

32. The image of the olive tree in Jer 11:16 is invoked in contrast to the fruitless fig tree. Note how the phrase is taken out of its threatening context in Jeremiah, where it actually is a quotation, and made to express hope and promise.

So it continues: **Amen, I say to you, that whichever one of you will say to this mountain** (Mark 11:23), that is, to Christ, who is the mountain sprung from the stone *cut without hands.*[33]

"Be lifted up and thrown into the sea, and does not doubt that whatever he **says will be done, it shall be done for him"** (Mark 11:23).

That is when the apostles will say: "Let us be worthily transferred to other nations, because *you have judged yourselves unworthy* to hear the word of God."[34]

The text continues: **And when you stand to pray, forgive if you have anything against anyone,** etc., as far as **your sins** (Mark 11:26).

Mark in his own way sums up the seven verses of the Lord's Prayer in one prayer. For whoever has had everything forgiven him, what else will he ask for, except that he might persevere in that which he has obtained?

And they come again to Jerusalem, etc. (Mark 11:27).

The elders say to him, *By what authority do you do these things?* Jesus answers them, "The baptism of John, *was it from heaven or from men?"* They considered and said, *We do not know* (Mark 11:23).[35] The hostile ones are shaded from the lamp, as it said, *I have prepared a lamp for my anointed; I shall clothe his enemies with shame.*[36] And Jesus says, "Neither will I tell you *by what authority* I do these things" (cf. Mark 11:33). Here God beats the perverted at their own game.[37]

33. Jerome *Dan* p. 932 411–413. The word "mountain" leads to another text, Dan 2:45, where the word occurs in relation to the powerful coming kingdom of God. This is understood to be Christ, and therefore "to the mountain" can be construed as "to Christ." To be precise about the Daniel text, it is the stone cut from the mountain that exhibits divine power. But the author needs the link with the mountain.

34. This text is connected with Acts 13:46, which is a decisive point in the argument developed in Paul's first missionary speech in Acts. It is possible that the mention of sea suggested the gentile world to the commentator.

35. Cf. Mark 11:27–33. The author presents the debate in summary form.

36. The commentator quotes Ps 132:17b–18a in an attempt to explain the attitude of the elders. The "anointed" (*christos* in Latin) represents Christ, who is all light, but the light does not illuminate his enemies.

37. The comment is actually an accommodation of Ps 18:26b, according to the Latin version known as the Roman Psalter. Literally it reads, "God is subverted with the perverted." I understand this as suggesting that God can be as cunning as his enemies.

CHAPTER 12

He began to speak to them in parables, etc. (Mark 12:1).

A man planted a vineyard. God is called a man, a father, to put it in a human way. The vineyard is the house of Israel, and the hedge is the protection of the angels. The pit for the winepress is the Law. The tower is the Temple. The farmers are the priests. The leaving on a journey on the part of God represents the freedom of our will. The servants sent are the prophets. The produce of the vineyard is obedience. Some of the prophets were flogged, others wounded, and others killed. The son, the most beloved and the final one, is the only begotten.

They will respect my son (Mark 12:6).

This is said in irony. And they threw him out of the vineyard, that is to say, out from the people, saying, *You are a Samaritan and have a demon.*[1] The vineyard is given to others, that is, to those who come from *east, west, south and north,* and who sit at table *with Abraham, Isaac, and Jacob, in the kingdom of* God.[2]

---

1. The verbal attack on Jesus in John 8:48 is quoted.
2. The allegory is christological and sketches the rejection of Jesus by the Jewish authorities. Some details are puzzling. The subjects of angels and free will do not fit comfortably into the overall pattern. That each nation had a guardian angel was standard patristic opinion based on Dan 10:13, 21. The arbitrariness of the interpretation in terms of free will is shown by the fact that another setting out on a journey, in Mark 13:34, is explained as

This rejected stone, which the corner supports, combines in a pure meal the lamb and bread.[3] He brings to a close the Old Testament and inaugurates the New. Here, like topaz, he presents wonders *to our eyes*.[4]

Then they question him with honeyed words. They surround him *like bees*,[5] which carry honey in the mouth, but have a sting in the tail, saying, *Master, we know that you are a truthful man*, etc. (Mark 12:14).[6]

Is it lawful to pay **tax to Caesar?**, etc. (Mark 12:14).

He replied to them who were holding the image of Caesar, "Give the coin to Caesar, as you are forced to, but give yourselves willingly to God" (cf. Mark 12:17). *The light of the face* of God, not of Caesar, *is marked as a sign upon us*.[7]

And Sadducees come **to him**, etc. (Mark 12:18).

We will discuss this question on another occasion. Another person's error is none of our business, except to say that human beings will be *like the angels* of God (cf. Mark 12:25), that is, no one dies there and no one is born there. There is neither young child nor old person.[8]

---

the body of Christ raised up to heaven. This suggests that free will was a subject on the author's mind. "Others" is glossed by using an amalgam citation of Matt 8:11 and Luke 13:29. The order of the directions is interesting for source analysis. Matthew has east and west, while Luke has east, west, north, and south. Today we rattle off the directions as "north, south, east, and west." (See further discussion at Mark 15:21.)

3. Cf. Ps 118:22–23. In a striking combination of imagery, the stone establishes the structure of a new dispensation in which the Passover meal (involving lamb and bread) is celebrated spiritually.

4. Cf. Ps 118:23. Sed *Car* I p. 37 288–289; Aug *Ps* 128 p. 1756 9; Euch *Ins* p. 148 11–13. Eucherius notes that some assert that the colors of all stones shine in topaz.

5. Ps 118:12.

6. The imagery of surrounding bees, honey, and sting derives from Ps 118:12a. The honeyed compliment is not honest but has a sting in the tail, because it is designed to harm.

7. The words of Jesus are paraphrased with an original and intelligent twist given to them. Ps 4:6b is also adapted to establish the absolute claim of God on us.

8. The author declares that since the question raised is based on a wrong idea, he does not wish to deal with it; it is not his problem. The manuscript history of the commentary shows that interpolations were made. At this point, a homily was inserted to remedy what seemed a deficiency in the mind of a later scribal editor. I have relegated this to an appendix. For a more detailed treatment see Michael Cahill, "The Identification of an Interpolated Homily in an Early Commentary on Mark."

Concerning the dead, do you not read in the Book of Moses about the bush, that they rise?[9] (Mark 12:26).

In this there is a likeness of you. In the bush a fire blazed, but it did not burn its thorns. Likewise, my words inflame you, and yet do not take away your thorns which have sprouted as a result of the curse.[10]

Saying, "I am the God of Abraham, and the God of Isaac, and the God of Jacob."

In naming God three times, he suggested the Trinity.[11]

He is not the God of the dead (Mark 12:27).

By repeating the one God, he indicates the single substance. For the ones who claim *the portion* they had chosen, they are the ones who are alive.[12] The dead are those who have lost what they claimed.[13]

And one of the scribes **asked him which was the first of all the commandments** (Mark 12:28).

He replied, *Hear, Israel, the Lord your God is the only God*, etc. (Mark 12:29). What is the problematic issue here, well known to all the experts in the Law, if not that the commandments are differently presented in Exodus, Leviticus and Deuteronomy?[14] For this reason, he established that there are two commandments, not one. Our infancy is nourished from these two breasts raised above the heart of the bride.[15]

9. Jesus is referring to Ex 3:2.

10. Cf. Gen 3:18. C. Arles *Ser* 95 p. 390 no. 374. The author makes a comparison between the burning bush and his listeners. This conforms to the purpose of the commentary as set out in the prologue. While there is a strong tone of oral delivery here, there are other indications that the work is a written composition.

11. The triad suggests the Trinity to the commentator. This willingness to see NT realities in the OT text is one of the features of precritical exegesis that causes most misgivings for modern Bible scholars. The Christian reading of the OT is one of the most debated topics in modern-day OT theology, e.g., Roger Brooks and John J. Collins, eds., *Hebrew Bible or Old Testament?*

12. Cf. Ps 142:5.

13. "Dead" and "alive" are taken in a spiritual sense. One is truly alive if one possesses God (cf. Ps 142:5). The author's comments on these words of Jesus ignore their role in the controversy which provoked them. This underlines the fact that the author chooses to pass over the matter without comment.

14. The author is referring to the versions of the Ten Commandments found in Ex 20:1–17 and Deut 5:6–21, while the love of neighbor commandment is found in Lev 19:18. The author invites us to see these two commandments as sources of life made available to us in the church, pictured as the bride.

15. Cf. Song 8:1.

And the scribe says to him, "You have spoken well, Master, in truth," etc. **And Jesus said to him, "You are not far from the kingdom of God"** (Mark 12:34).

How is it that he is not far, when he comes with expertise? Because ignorance is farther from the kingdom of God than knowledge. Therefore, to the Sadducees (above) he says, "You are in error, you do not know *the Scriptures nor the power of God*" (Mark 12:24).

And Jesus was teaching them in the temple (cf. Mark 12:35), that is, he speaks openly to them about himself *so that they would be without excuse.*[16] He did this so that fire would ignite the dry models of the scribes and of the Pharisees, *who like to walk in long robes*, etc. (Mark 12:38). They receive *a greater judgment* (cf. Mark 12:40).[17]

And Jesus, sitting opposite the treasury, that is the place where valuables were kept safe (Mark 12:41).

He was observing how the *rich people were throwing in plenty* (cf. Mark 12:41). And a poor widow came and put in two small coins, worth about a quarter.[18] He said to his disciples, *This poor widow put in more than anyone* (Mark 12:43).[19]

Who are the rich if not those who contribute from the treasure of their heart *new things and old*, namely *the unclear and hidden elements of the wisdom* of both Testaments?[20] Who indeed is the poor woman if not myself and those like me?[21] I put in what I can, and aspire to that which I cannot explain to you. As you have heard, God notices not how much but from how much.[22] Everyone is able to contribute their quarter's worth. This is the loaf of bread in Leviticus, which stands for a ready will.[23] Why is this said to be a "quarter"? This is be-

---

16. Cf. Rom 1:20.

17. The mention of the Pharisees is taken from the parallel passage in Matt 22:2–13. According to the prologue, the material of the Gospels includes examples or models. Some are dry and useless and deserve to be burned (cf. Jude 7).

18. Cf. Luke 21:2.

19. The difficult term is correctly but very briefly explained. The Latin *quadrans* indicates a quarter of a standard unit of currency. The author's subsequent comments demand that the idea of "quarter" be preserved in translation.

20. The truly rich are those with spiritual contributions to make. Ps 51:6b and Matt 13:52 are used to evoke the Bible scholar of the first line of the prologue who can explain both testaments.

21. Again, as in the prologue, he compares himself to the poor widow.

22. Greg *Hom* 5 1093 C; Cyprian *Op* p. 64 292.

23. Cf. 2 Cor 8:11. Lev 2 contains a detailed description of the sacrificial cereal offering (cf. Ex 29:23; Num 6:19). The spiritual interior attitude of will, entailed in sacrifice, is singled out for mention. But why the cereal offering is specified is not evident.

cause it consists of three things: thought, word, and deed.[24] What does it mean to say "she put in *her entire sustenance*"? (Mark 12:44). What the body wants above all is sustenance. For that reason it is said, "All *the work of man* is in his mouth."[25]

24. The author returns to the sum of money donated by the widow, described in Roman currency as a *quadrans*, a quarter. A unit of coins, weights, or measures was divided into twelve parts. A quarter was therefore made up of three smaller parts. Thus the author appears to categorize the gift of the widow as a sacrifice by the reference to the cereal offering in Leviticus. He then points out that a perfect sacrifice is made up of thought, word, and deed. It has been suggested that the Irish trait of arranging things in triads is possibly to be recognized here (Maura Walsh and Dáibhí Ó Cróinín, *Cummian's Letter*, p. 221). Another triad is found at the end of chapter 14, the three stages of temptation. Though Roman coins have been found in Ireland, it is unlikely that their use was so common as to allow a metaphor based on an understanding of Roman currency to be pastorally viable; the term *quadrans* itself would have been intelligible to those with knowledge of Latin.

25. The commentator draws out the meaning of Jesus' words by reminding us that self-preservation is the first law and instinct. He paraphrases Eccles 6:7a in support. The widow's offering was total.

CHAPTER 13

And when he was leaving the temple, etc. (Mark 13:1).

He spells out for the disciples the disaster of the end time, that is, the destruction of the temple, together with the people and its Scripture, of which not a stone would be left upon a stone. This refers to the testimonies of the prophets concerning those about whom the Jews twisted them as in the case of Absalom, Ezra, Zerubabel, and the Maccabees.[1] The things he enumerates are all to be despised rather than investigated: false christs, false prophets, nation against nation, kingdom against kingdom, earthquakes, the beating of preachers as the gospel is preached to the ends of the earth, so that before the Judg-

---

1. The physical destruction of Jerusalem ("not a stone upon a stone") is applied to a controversial issue in ancient biblical hermeneutics. The commentator is vigorously rejecting the Antiochene School of psalm exegesis, which reads the Psalms historically, i.e., in relation to the times of David and Absalom, the Restoration, and the Maccabees. He dismisses this approach as "Jewish." By "prophets" the author is referring to the writers of the Psalms, which are viewed as prophetical writings. While it may not be apparent at first sight, the commentator is actually launching a strong attack on a method of psalm exegesis which he abhors. The Antiochene School represented, in the early centuries of the church's biblical interpretation, the historical and literal approach to the Old Testament. By contrast, Origen in the east and Augustine in the west, followed by Cassiodorus, for example, interpreted the Psalms as messianic, i.e., prophesying about Jesus Christ. For a full discussion of this issue in relation to authorship of the Markan Commentary, see Michael Cahill, "Is the First Commentary on Mark an Irish Work?" (pp. 38–42). In no source have I been able to note a mention of Ezra, as found in the Gospel commentary. Perhaps the original "Ezra" was a slip for "Ezechias," who features in the other texts.

ment the church may cry out, *From the ends of the earth I have cried out to you,*
Lord.[2]

Members of the same household will rise against each other, the abomina-
tion in the temple, the flight to the mountains; he who ascends to the heights
let him not descend to the depths. *Pray that your flight does not take place* in winter *or on the sabbath,*[3] that is, so that the fruits of our work are not terminated
with the end of time. For winter brings an end to fruit, and time ceases on the
sabbath.[4] There will be great *tribulation,*[5] and short days for the sake of the chosen
ones, lest the wickedness of this age should alter their understanding, as is said
about Enoch.[6]

After these things the sun will be darkened for hearts cold as in winter. The
moon will not shine clear at a time of storm of dissensions. And the stars will
fade in light when there will be almost no descendants of Abraham, to whom
they have been likened.[7]

And the powers in the heavens will be moved to a punishing anger (cf. Mark
13:25), when they will be sent by the Son of Man coming *on the clouds* with
power (cf. Mark 13:26). He is the one who previously came down in an unas-
suming manner like the dew on the fleece of Gideon.[8] *And he will gather the*
chosen ones from the four winds, (cf. Mark 13:27), like winnowed wheat from the
threshing floor of the entire earth.[9]

The parable of the fig tree is this prophecy: the sprouting *leaves* signify the
words we have just looked at. Indeed, the onset of *summer* represents the Day
of Judgment when every tree will show what it is made of, whether it is dry

2. Despite the inevitable suffering accompanying the work of evangelization (Mark
13:9–10), the commentator hopes that the words of Ps 61:2 will be literally fulfilled.

3. Cf. Matt 24:20.

4. Note how the similar parallel text, Matt 24:20, is confused with Mark 13:18. Winter
and sabbath both suspend normal operations. A spiritual message is drawn. As the working
week provides time to work, but is suspended on the sabbath, so our time on earth for
doing good is limited.

5. Cf. Matt 24:21.

6. Cf. Heb 11:5. The author suggests a reason for God's intervention in limiting the
tribulation. Surrounding evil can affect a person's understanding.

7. Cf. Gen 15:5. The changes in the sun, moon, and stars (Mark 13:24–25) are interpreted in terms of the situation of the church in the world.

8. Aug *Ps* 71 p. 978 9; Amb *Sp* p. 17 447–458; C. Arles *Ser* 117 p. 489 25. The text is
paraphrased so that the control of the Son of Man over the powers is affirmed. The dew on
the fleece (Judges 6:37–38) was seen in the exegetical tradition as a type of Mary conceiv-
ing Jesus. Just as the dew was unique, so is the mystery of the Incarnation. The author
points up the gentle nature of the event in contrast to the second coming.

9. Cf. Ezek 22:15; 36:19. C. Arles *Ser* 209 p. 836.

for burning, or green for planting in Eden with the tree of life.[10] The leaves of the tree will bring salvation to the gentiles,[11] referring to the words in which he will say, *Come, blessed of my Father*, etc.[12]

Thus the text continues, **Heaven and earth will pass away but my words will not.** Concerning that day and the hour, **no one knows, neither the angels in heaven nor the Son, only the Father** (cf. Mark 13:31).

What does it mean to say, *nor the Son, only the Father?* What does *nor the son* mean? Concerning whom it is said, *The Father is greater than me*, that is, greater than his body situated on earth, which is the church.[13]

Watch and pray, for you know not when the time may be (Mark 13:33).

Watching is an activity of the soul before the death of the body. The man setting out on a journey represents the body of Christ raised up to heaven. He leaves his home which is the church and gives to his servants their respective responsibilities, namely five talents, according to Matthew, or ten pounds, according to Luke.[14]

He orders the doorkeeper to be on watch (cf. Mark 13:34).

This refers to the preacher to whom it is said, "If you do not announce to the evil person the evil he is doing, then *I will require his blood from your hand.*"[15]

---

10. Cf. Gen 2:9.

11. Cf. Rev 22:2.

12. The text says that there is a parable to be found in the growth of the tree. The point of the parable is termed a "prophecy," a message of spiritual value. The leaves are taken to refer to the words under examination, namely, the warnings about the end of time. In other words, the leaves signal summer as the cosmic signs signal the end. The condition of the tree in summer determines the eventual harvest.

The leaves of the tree are identified with those of the trees in Rev 22:2. The leaves are now taken to represent a different set of words, namely, Matt 25:34. The combining of the Markan text with the two other texts to make a statement about the evangelization of the gentiles is symptomatic of the author's interest in this topic.

13. This apparent limitation of the knowledge of Jesus was stressed by the Arians, and so this was a much debated text. The author quotes John 14:28b, which at first sight seems to buttress the subordinationist view of the Son. He explains that the comparison is with the church on earth.

14. Cf. Matt 25:14–30; cf. Luke 19:11–27. The version in Mark 13:34 is very brief and succinct. In chapter 12 the setting out on a journey was understood as a pointer to free will. Here, the application to the Ascension is part of an ecclesial interpretation. The church as the body of Christ on earth has been entrusted with gifts and duties.

15. He fails to note that the instruction to the doorkeeper is proper to Mark. He quotes Ezek 3:18 (Old Latin version) as a comment on the verse, seeing the doorkeeper as a preacher.

Watch, therefore, etc. (Mark 13:35).

In the evening or at midnight when the firstborn of the Egyptians were killed.[16]

Lest **he finds you asleep** (cf. Mark 13:36).

For whoever sleeps sees not real objects but imaginings. He watches in vain for those things he has seen. That is certainly the situation of those whom the love of the world bears away. What they dreamt about as certain, deserts them after this life.[17]

The text continues, **What I say to you, I say to all, Be watchful** (Mark 13:37).

With this ending he concludes the speech, so that *the last* may hear from *the first* the common property of all the commandments.[18]

---

16. The allusion to Ex 12:29 is facilitated because the tradition liked to link up in a string of association such items as midnight events. There is no intrinsic reason for the allusion, although the grim nature of the event suits the threatening tone of the discourse.

17. The commentator draws a parallel between sleep and lack of vigilance. The inattentive Christian who gets too absorbed in this world is like the person who hankers after what he has only dreamed about. This world is equally unreal in the sense that it will not endure.

18. Cf. Mark 10:31 and par.

CHAPTER 14

❧

Now the Pasch of the Unleavened Bread was two days later (Mark 14:1).

Now, let us sprinkle our book with blood just like the doorposts of the houses.[1] Let us put a scarlet thread around "the house of our prayer."[2] Like Zerah, let us tie a scarlet thread on our hand.[3] So we may be able to tell the story of the red heifer slaughtered in the valley.[4]

"Pasch" means "a passing over"; "Pesach" is a sacrifice.[5] In the sacrifice of the lamb, and in the passing of the people through the sea, or of the angel

---

1. Ex 12:22. There follows a list of elements making up the feast of Passover, with explanations of various kinds. The author seems to be following a source other than Ex 12:1–28 because items such as the full moon do not occur there.

2. Cf. Josh 2:18. The author uses a phrase of Augustine's (Aug *Ps* 130 p. 1899 no. 3 4–5).

3. Cf. Gen 38:27–30.

4. Cf. Num 19:1–11. The author invites us to imaginatively enter into the appropriate mood for studying the account of the passion and death of Jesus. The color red or scarlet is the link. The blood of the lamb saves the Israelites in Ex 12:22. Note the reference to the book; an author is writing. In Josh 2:18 Rahab is saved by the sign of the cord. The thread on Zerah's hand in Gen 38:27–30 guarantees firstborn rights. Christ is compared to the red cow in Num 19:1–11 insofar as both have a purification-sacrifice value. Jean Daniélou suggests from the evidence of the Letter of Barnabas and of 1 Clement that some very early Christian *testimonia* (collections of Scripture texts) centered on the term "scarlet" came into existence (*The Theology of Jewish Christianity*, pp. 99–101).

5. Cf. 2 Chron 35:11; Deut 16:2. The Hebrew word for Passover survives in two forms in the Latin Vulgate: *Pascha* and *Phase*. Both are derived from the Hebrew, the former via

through Egypt, the passion of Christ is prefigured, along with the redemption of the people from hell, when he visited us *after two days*.[6]

That is to say, when the moon is at its fullest, when the age of Christ has been completed, in order that we may have no dark part when we eat the flesh of the immaculate lamb *who takes away the sins of the world*.[7] We eat in one house, *the only one of her mother, the chosen*, the catholic church.[8] We are shod with charity and armed with virtue.[9] We say, *Indeed our Passover has been sacrificed*.[10]

And the chief priests and the scribes were looking for, etc. (Mark 14:1).
Iniquity has gone forth from the leaders in *Babylon*.[11] Once the head has been killed the whole body is weakened. And so the wretched people carry out what the leaders initiate. They avoid the festival. This is appropriate for them because there is no festivity for those who have lost life and mercy.

Jesus comes to Bethany (cf. Mark 14:2). He always returns to his own bed, as does the young stag.[12] That is, the Son of the Father, *obedient unto death*, asks obedience of us.[13] Simon the leper signifies, in the first place, the faithless world and, subsequently, the faithful one. The woman with the alabaster jar stands for the church with faith, which says, *My nard gives forth its fragrance*.[14] The nard is termed *pure*,[15] that is to say mystical and precious. *The house was filled with*

---

the Greek, the latter directly. The commentator uses both terms. It is difficult to shift his explanation into an English language context. His comment makes better sense if the underlying etymology is more clearly expressed by using the form "pesach" instead of "phase."

6. The "Harrowing of Hell" is brought to the author's mind by way of the phrase "after two days" (Hos 6:2), which dated, traditionally, Christ's visit to the underworld. Another reference to Christ's descent into Hell occurs at the end of chapter 14.

7. Cf. John 1:29; 1:36; cf. John 6:53. The brightness of the moon is taken as a symbol of spiritual readiness. A similar phrase is used in *Catechesis Celtica* (André Wilmart, "Catécheses Celtiques," p. 46, 14–15). The date of Easter was determined by lunar calculations and, as we will see, was a matter of bitter controversy.

8. Cf. Ex. 12:3; cf. Song 6:8. The term "catholic" is used to differentiate from Arian.
9. Cf. Ex 12:11.
10. 1 Cor 5:7. Jerome *Ep* 15 p. 64 1–3; 22 p. 204 8–9; *Hom* pp. 536–537.

11. The author compares the priests and scribes to the wicked men who intrigue against Susanna (Dan 13:5). Corruption in the leadership affects everyone. His interest in the quality of leadership comes through again. Their reluctance to act on the feast day (Mark 14:2) is explained spiritually.

12. Greg *Hom* 23 1243 D; *Cant* p. 40 776–777. Gregory the Great in a homily on the Lukan parallel identifies Jesus as a stag. Possibly the phrase *super montes Bether* ("upon the mountains of Bether") in the Vulgate text of Song 2:17, was associated with Bethany.

13. Cf. Phil 2:8. Jerome *Nom* p. 135 27. The etymology of Bethany as "the house of obedience" (as in Jerome) suggests the theme of obedience.

14. Song 1:11.
15. Cf. John 12:3.

perfume,[16] that is, heaven and earth. The broken alabaster jar represents carnal desire, which is shattered at *the head, from which the whole body* has been joined together.[17] He himself is lying down, that is lowering himself so that the faith of the sinful woman might touch him. She goes up from the feet to the head and comes down through faith *from the head*[18] to the feet, that is to say, to Christ and his members.[19]

Some were indignant (Mark 14:4).

We have here a synecdoche, when one is taken for many and many for one.[20] They said to one another, *Why this waste* of oil? The one who wasted salvation found the waste, just as he encounters the snare of death in a fruit-bearing fig tree.[21] The ointment is said to have been bought for 300 hundred denarii, and it is to be *given to the poor* (Mark 14:5).

He speaks of the mystery of faith under the guise of avarice. Indeed our faith is bought for 300 denarii, that is the ten senses multiplied by three, for the body, soul, and spirit. So let us, poor in spirit, like Gideon taking men to the number of 300, destroy the camp of the foreigners with our broken jars, and with our trumpets and torches. And like Abraham with 300 men, let us divide the spoil toward evening.[22]

The text continues: **She has performed a good deed upon me** (Mark 14:6).

16. Cf. John 12:3.
17. Cf. Eph 4:16.
18. Cf. Ps 133:2.
19. The commentator combines the "head" in Mark 14:3 (= Matt 26:7) with the "feet" of Luke 7:38 and John 12:3. The association of "oil" and "head" evokes the oil flowing down from Aaron's head (Ps 133:2). The pun on "members" survives in translation.
20. Aug *Pet* p. 153 3–4. The commentator is explaining why Mark and Matthew have the plural, when in John 12:4, Judas alone is specified as the one complaining.
21. The author attempts to explain the paradox that Judas could not find salvation in the Savior. Some birds are trapped and killed in a fruit tree. The same term, *laqueus*, is used in Matt 27:5, when Judas hanged himself.
22. Origen *Lev* 3.7 p. 150. The five physical senses are matched by five spiritual. The triple division (cf. 1 Thess 5:23) is on a different base but the author needs the figure 300. The makeup of the human person is not peculiar to the author. The notion of five spiritual senses goes back to Origen. The number 300 acts as a thread linking stories of Gideon (Judges 7:16–22) and Abraham. The latter presents problems. Gen 14:14 has 318 men, while Gen 49:27 has Benjamin dividing the spoil toward evening. Curiously, a text of Origen combines the references to Judges 7:16 and Gen 14:14 and, likewise, has 300 not 318 (*In Gen Hom* 2 172 A). The general point of the author seems to be that our entire being must be dedicated to the pursuit of the mystery of faith.

Whoever believes in God gets credit *for righteousness.*[23] It is one thing to believe him, it is another thing to believe in him, that is to cast your entire self upon him.[24]

She did what she could (Mark 14:8), not something else, so that we may not despise what is within our ability.

She has anointed my body in advance (Mark 14:8).

That is, before he came to hinder, namely Judas Iscariot. He was one of the Twelve; one numerically, but not one by merit; one in name, but not one in will; one in body, but not one in soul. As the bridegroom sings to the bride, *You have wounded my heart, my sister, bride . . . with one of your eyes, with one hair of your neck.* The eye and the hair represent the power of wisdom.[25] Because to Judas along with the others, it is said, *To you it has been given to know the mystery of the kingdom,* and *I have given you power,* etc.[26]

He went off to the leaders after Satan went out into him.[27] This is a case of where *night declares knowledge to night.*[28] Birds of a feather flock together.[29] Mary ran to the apostles as *day utters the word to day,* and Judas to the Jews as *night declares knowledge to night.*[30] They promise money and lose life. He receives the money as he loses life. *He was seeking an opportunity.*[31] However, an opportunity of trickery is never found, so that he may not be excused here nor there.[32]

---

23. Cf. Gen 15:6.

24. Cf. Gen 15:6 (= Rom 4:3). The explanation is concerned with this text rather than Mark. It further develops the theme of faith pursued by the author in this section of the commentary.

25. The quotation of Song 4:9 is difficult to situate in its new context, but it possibly relates to Mary's wiping Jesus' feet with her hair as found in the Luke and John parallels. How eye and hair represent wisdom is not explained. The term "wounded" is taken out of context, giving the sense that Judas as a member of the church, the bride, has wounded Jesus by betrayal.

26. Mark 4:11a; Luke 10:19.

27. Cf. John 13:27. This reads awkwardly, but the textual witnesses are unanimous.

28. Ps 19:2b.

29. I translate the Latin idiom with an equivalent English one.

30. Ps 19:2b and 2a. Cf. Mark 16:10. Euch *Ins* pp. 90 22–91 3. The use of the Psalter text is ingenious but fanciful. Eucherius uses the same psalm text in a somewhat similar manner to contrast the action of Judas and the subsequent work of the apostles.

31. Luke 22:6 and par.

32. The parallel Luke 22:6 is quoted and not Mark 14:11b. The assertion that no opportunity is found is puzzling since, in fact, Judas did betray. Maybe the author means that no wrong was done by Jesus to provide a legal and just pretext for Jesus' death, which would have vindicated Judas.

He commits himself to betray. As his master, the devil, was saying previously, *I will give you all this power.*[33]

And on the first day of the Feast of the Unleavened Bread (Mark 14:12).

The unleavened bread is eaten with bitterness. The bread represents for us our redemption, indeed the bitterness is the passion of Christ.[34]

The disciples say, "Where do you want us to go?"

May we direct our steps according to the will of God.[35] The Lord makes known with whom he would eat the Passover, and according to his custom he sends a pair, as we have explained above.[36]

And he said, "Go into the city," etc. (Mark 14:13).

The city represents what is surrounded by walls of faith.[37] The man they meet represents the original people.[38] The man carrying the jar of water stands for the law of the letter.[39]

---

33. Luke 4:6a. The words of the devil to Jesus are quoted to show up the sin of Judas as a deal with the devil.

34. The linking of the bread with sorrow is not found in the Bible and indicates the influence of later Jewish Passover ritual, in which the bitter herbs and salt water symbolize the sufferings and the sorrow. Christians celebrate their Passover conscious of the sufferings of Jesus.

35. Ps 37:23.

36. See at Mark 11:1.

37. The city is understood as walled. This indicates awareness that Jerusalem was walled or that the early medieval town was walled. A walled city would not have been part of the seventh-century Irish writer's experience except through travel in Europe or through study.

38. Greg Il *Trac* p. 21 56. The commentator shows an interest in the *populus primitivus*. Here it refers to the Jewish community, but in the earlier cases it means the early Christian church:

- "The first church [*primitiva ecclesia*] is constructed from these four cornerstones" (at Mark 1:15);
- "The home they come to is the early church" (*primitiva est ecclesia*), at Mark 3:20;
- "The ship is like the church at its beginning" (*puppis initium ecclesiae est*) at Mark 4:38;
- "This refers to the church in its early and later stages" (*ecclesiam primam*) at Mark 6:1;
- "The seven basketfuls are the first seven churches" (*primae septem ecclesiae*) at Mark 8:8.

There are references to the early church community in Hiberno-Latin biblical writings, but a characteristic of this tradition is that it commonly refers to the holy family of Jesus, Mary, and Joseph (see Glenn W. Olsen, "Reference to the Ecclesia Primitiva in Eighth Century Irish Gospel Exegesis"; cf. Glenn Olsen, "The Idea of the Ecclesia Primitiva," esp. pp. 66–70).

39. Cf. Rom 7:6; cf. 2 Cor 3:6. The man with the jar of water stands for the Jewish people, who, from the author's perspective, ignore the real Christian meaning of the Scriptures. There are frequent remarks about the Jewish interpretation of the Scriptures in the commentary.

Follow him, etc. (Mark 14:13).

He leads on high where *the dining room* of Christ is (cf. Mark 14:14).[40] That is why Rahab instructs the spies not to travel in the lowlands but to take to the heights. The *large dining room* is the great church, in which the name of the Lord is spoken,[41] furnished as it is with a variety of powers and languages, as in the text, *with varied clothing.*[42] Here the Passover is prepared for the Lord. The ruler of the house is the apostle Peter, to whom the Lord entrusts his house so that there may be *one faith* under one shepherd.[43]

When it was evening, etc. (Mark 14:17).

The evening of the day points to the evening of the world.[44] For *around the eleventh hour* come the *last* who are the *first* to get the coin of eternal life,[45] because before the cross Abraham was in hell, and after the cross the thief is in paradise.[46]

And as they were eating, he said to them, **"One of you who is eating with me will betray me"** (Mark 14:18).

So that what is said might be fulfilled: *He who ate my bread gloried in his usurpation of me.*[47] All are touched just like a chord struck on a harp. All the strings, well tautened, reply in harmony, *Is it I, Lord?*[48] One, negligent and intoxicated by the love of money,[49] said, *Is it I, Rabbi?*[50] And he says to them, *One of the twelve* (Mark 14:20). The wolf isolates the sheep that he seizes. The sheep that

40. The Latin term for "dining room" (*cenaculum*) can also mean "an upper room," and this permits a textual parallel to be seen with the advice of Rahab in Josh 2:16.

41. Cf. Ps 23:22; cf. Ex 9:16.

42. Cf. Ps 45:14. The church's mission is to proclaim God's name (cf. Ps 23:22). Because of its geographical spread among the nations, this is done in various languages (cf. Ps 45:14).

43. Corresponding to the earlier references to the mother church of Rome is the mention of Petrine primacy. Cf. Eph 4:5; John 10:16.

44. The author shares the mood of imminent doom that is characteristic of writers at this time. I note a fairly close similarity in *Catechesis Celtica* (*Cat. Celt.* p. 35, 5–6) with the Matthean parallel. Evening is to be understood mystically as the end time of the world because Christ suffered almost at the end of time. The parable in Matt 20:1–16 is applied to those who live close to the moment of salvation. Another illustration is offered, of Abraham and of the thief (Luke 23:43), who are contrasted. Abraham worked in the vineyard early, but the thief came at the eleventh hour.

45. Cf. Matt 20:1–16.

46. Cf. Luke 23:43.

47. Ps 41:9.

48. Matt 26:22. Greg *Reg* p. 260 13–22; *Cat. Celt.* p. 35 13–14. The reaction of the disciples is described in an expressive musical metaphor. I have also noted it in Gregory, though in a different context (*Pastoral Care*, p. 89).

49. Cf. John 12:6.

50. Matt 26:25.

leaves the fold is exposed to the bites of the wolf.[51] The Son of Man goes but woe to the man by whom he will be betrayed (cf. Mark 14:21). Many, like Judas, do good, but it is of utterly no advantage to them.[52]

It would have be better for him if he had not born, if he had remained hidden in his mother's womb (cf. Mark 14:21). Better never to exist than to face torments.[53]

Jesus took the bread, and saying the blessing, broke it (Mark 14:22).

He transfigures his body into the bread.[54] The bread is the present church. It is accepted in faith, blessed in number, broken in sufferings, given in examples, taken in teachings. He turns his blood into a chalice mixed with wine and water. As we are purged of our sins by one, we will be redeemed from our punishments by the other. For by the blood of the lamb the houses are preserved from the blow of the angel, and by the water of the Red Sea, the enemies are wiped out.[55] These represent the ministries of the church of Christ.[56]

Giving thanks, he gave it to them (Mark 14:23).

It is by grace and not by merits that we are saved by God.[57]

---

51. Cf. John 10:12.

52. Presumably the author is thinking of the good actions done by Judas before his fall from grace.

53. The comment is reminiscent of Job 3.

54. The formula used in regard to the body and blood of the Lord is unusual, but by no means unique. The subject has been studied, with particular attention to the Hiberno-Latin literature, by Martin McNamara in "The Inverted Eucharistic Formula." I have noted a similar usage in *Catechesis Celtica*: *offerens corpus et sanguinen suum in panem et vinum* (*Cat. Celt.* p. 35 2). If the bread becomes his body, then his body has to change to bread, in some sense. The bread is taken as symbol of the church. He finds parallels in our experience of church with the series of verbs taken from the institution narrative. Jean Rittmueller has provided a detailed discussion of the use of this section of the commentary in a later Irish Gospel commentary (See "The Gospel Commentary of Máel Brigte," esp. pp. 196–198).

55. The wine and water are given an allegorical meaning. Just as the blood of the lamb (Ex 11–12) protected the Israelites, so the blood of Jesus redeems us; as the water of the Red Sea destroyed the Egyptians (Ex 14), so the water washes away our sins. The latter image extends to the water of Baptism.

56. The liturgical celebration of the two sacraments of Baptism and Eucharist are both "mysteries" and "ministries," and the common scribal confusion of the terms in the manuscript tradition corresponds to the overlap in meaning. A comparable text, where both terms, along with water and wine, are closely associated, is found in *Adomnan's Life of Columba* (section 53a, p. 324; see also the editors' discussion of the terms in the index, s.v. "misterium," pp. 587–588).

57. The element of "giving" is used by the commentator to remind his readers that grace is a gift.

And they all drank from it (Mark 14:23).

Even Judas drinks though he is not filled and he does not extinguish the thirst caused by the eternal fire,[58] because he takes the mysteries of Christ unworthily.[59] Here is displayed a stain on *wool* which will never be removed;[60] a sacrifice in any place whatever does not cleanse it. The blood of the New Testament, which *is shed for many*, does not cleanse all (cf. Mark 14:24).

I will not drink of the fruit of the vine until the day, etc. (Mark 14:25).

This changes only the sacrifice and not the time, so that we never conduct the Lord's Supper before the fourteenth moon. Because whoever conducts the resurrection on the fourteenth, conducts the Lord's Supper on the eleventh moon, and this is never found in the Old, nor in the New Testament.[61]

A hymn having been sung, etc. (Mark 14:26)

That is, in praise of the Lord, such as in the psalm, *Those who seek him will praise the Lord,* and *they have eaten, and all the prosperous of the earth have adored.*[62]

---

58. Cf. Luke 16:24.

59. Cf. 1 Cor 11:27. The author accepts that Judas participated in the Supper, though the extent to which he did has always been the subject of controversy. The term used in Latin for "mysteries" is *mysteria.*

60. Cf. Is 1:18. Greg *Hom* 10 1111 C.

61. The statement of Jesus about when he will drink the wine leads to a polemical statement about the date of Easter. The explanation given is dense. The author argues from the sequence of days. If Easter Sunday ("resurrection") were to be on the fourteenth day of lunar calculation, then the Last Supper ("Passover") would be on the eleventh. There is no basis, he argues, for having the Passover (OT and NT forms) before the fourteenth. Therefore, Easter cannot be before the fourteenth, since it must be three days later (after the Supper). This is the most discussed passage of the commentary among scholars. It brings us to the heart of one of the burning controversies in the Latin church in the early Middle Ages. It assumed a long-running and bitter quality in the Irish and British churches, between the "conservatives" wishing to retain the old ways and the "progressives" who wanted to conform to the Roman dating. A recent discussion of the issue is provided by the editors of Cummian's letter "De Controversia Paschali" ("Concerning the Controversy about Easter"). The question of common authorship of commentary and letter is involved (See Maura Walsh and Dáibhí Ó Cróinín, *Cummian's Letter,* pp. 25–29, 68).

The older custom, found among some Irish churches, for example, saw Easter as the Christian Passover and thus followed the Jewish custom of celebrating it on the fourteenth day of the month Nisan, whatever the day of the week. The rest of the church celebrated it on the following Sunday. This is the basis of the problem, but it is a very complex issue because of the host of different systems devised to perform the dating calculations. I note a parallel in *Catechesis Celtica: Vespere dicit XIIII lunae . . . in pasca legale celebrans* (*Cat. Celt.* p. 35, 5).

62. Ps 22:26a, 29a. The same psalm is quoted in the same context in *Cat. Celt.* p. 38, 113.

And **they went out to the Mount of Olives.**

Jesus is arrested on Mount Olivet, and from there he ascends to heaven. This is so that we may realize that we ascend to heaven from the place where we keep vigil, pray, and are bound, and also, that we should not resist on earth.[63]

All of you will experience scandal (Mark 14:27).

All fall, but not all stay down. *Does he that sleeps rise again no more?*[64] It is human to fall but diabolical to stay down.

It is written: *Strike the shepherd.*[65] The prophet calls for the passion of the Lord. The Father responds, *I will strike the shepherd* (Mark 14:27). Because of the prayers of those in hell,[66] the Son is sent by the Father and is struck, that is to say, he becomes incarnate and he suffers. *The sheep will be scattered* (Mark 14:27), with the seizure of the shepherd. The resurrection is promised, lest hope be extinguished.

Peter says, "Even if all are scandalized," etc. (Mark 14:29).

A bird without feathers tries to fly high. However, the very body weighs down the soul, just as the fear of the Lord is often overcome by the fear of human death.

Before the cock crows, you will deny me three times (Mark 14:30).

The cock crows twice, and Peter denies three times.[67] The cock is the herald of the light. Who is this if not the Holy Spirit? Through the voice of the Holy Spirit, in prophecy and in the apostles, we are aroused from the threefold denial by which we have denied God. We, frightened by the voice of servant girls, are stirred to most bitter tears after failures. We have thought badly about God, we have spoken badly against our neighbors, and we have done badly by ourselves.

63. The author gives a quick preview of the agony and arrest of Jesus in the Garden, and of his subsequent Ascension from nearby. He makes spiritual applications to the lives of later disciples.

64. Ps 41:8; cf. Is 24:20.

65. The author cites the original form of Zech 13:7, which allows him to regard the adapted form in the Gospel text as the voice of God the Father. Note the efficacy attributed to the prayers of the OT just ones (cf. on Mark 5:23). The identification of Jesus as a shepherd is not commented on. It is not clear that, in the mind of the author, the agency of the Father is to be extended to the striking.

66. I have used this translation to preserve the reminiscence of the creed's "he descended into hell."

67. The mss give a variety of numbers, and the Vulgate text is likewise variously attested. The Gospels' inconsistency is the basic reason for the uncertainty.

And they come to the farm of Gethsemane (Mark 14:32).

That is, "the valley of fatness", where *fat bulls encircled* him and *many calves* surrounded him.[68]

Sit here while I pray (Mark 14:32).

He is isolated in prayer who is isolated in suffering, because he prays and they sleep, weighed down by heaviness of heart.[69]

He began to fear, and he said, **"My soul is sad even to death"** (Mark 14:33–34).

We are taught to be troubled and sad before the judgment of death. It is only through him, and not of ourselves, that we can say, *the prince of this world is coming; he has no power over me.*[70]

And he said, "Abba, Father" (Mark 14:36).

He speaks in Hebrew and Greek, because *there is no distinction between Jew and Greek.*[71]

If possible,[72] take this cup from me, but not what I wish (cf. Mark 14:36).

To the finish, he does not cease from teaching us to obey our fathers and to prefer their wishes to our own.

He found them asleep (Mark 14:37).

As they sleep spiritually, so they sleep bodily.

Watch and pray, lest you enter into temptation (Mark 14:38).

Whoever neglects to pray, enters into temptation. Three times the disciples sleep and three times the Lord prays and wakes them up. The three periods of sleep represent the three dead persons that the Lord awakened: the first in the

---

68. Jerome *Nom* p. 136 22. His explanation is the same as Jerome's. The term "fat" leads to another biblical text with that word and, with an appropriate suggestion of danger, Ps 22:12 (inverted and accommodated).

69. Literally, the author refers to their "fatness" of heart.

70. We are to fear the judgment at the moment of death (Cf. Sir 41:3a), but, if we unite ourselves to Jesus, we will be empowered to be defiant and confident, as we see him in John 14:30.

71. Aug *Ev* p. 285 1–3. He quotes from Rom 10:12 to suggest that this was the reason that Jesus used the languages. The alleged use of the two languages is interesting. This is a statement made from the point of view of someone commenting on the Greek text of the Gospel, since the Greek is not visible in the Latin. This may indicate that the author is following another's commentary here. There is a close parallel in Augustine.

72. Matt 26:39.

house, the second near the tomb, and the third from the tomb.[73] The three periods of vigil of the Lord teach us to keep the Three Persons in mind when we pray. It also teaches us to ask pardon for past, future, and present things.[74]

Judas comes **with swords and clubs** (cf. Mark 14:43).

He who despairs of the help of God relies on this world's power. He gives the sign of a kiss with the poison of deceit, just as Cain offered a deceitful and rejected sacrifice.[75] That is why they offer wine with vinegar on the cross.[76]

And they seized Jesus (Mark 14:46).

Here is Joseph in bonds, *sold* by his brothers.[77] *And the iron pierced his soul.*[78] One man *drew a sword* (Mark 14:47), and cut off the ear of a servant. The preaching of Peter cut off from the Jews the hearing of the Kingdom of God.[79]

Then all his disciples abandoned him and took flight (Mark 14:50).

Then what is said is fulfilled, *You have taken away friend and neighbor, and you have taken away my acquaintances, from misery.*[80]

A certain youth was following him wearing a linen cloth over his nude body **and they seized him. However he let go of the cloth, and escaped from them in the nude** (cf. Mark 14:51–52).

This is proper to Mark. This is like the case of Joseph, who leaving behind his tunic, fled in the nude from the hands of the shameless mistress of the house.

73. Cf. Mark 5:41; Luke 7:14; John 11:44.

74. The author offers three allegories of the triad. The three raised are the daughter of Jairus (Mark 5:41), the widow's son (Luke 7:14), and Lazarus (John 11:44). There is an earlier similar treatment in Gregory (*Iob* 4 p. 196 52) and a parallel in *Cat. Celt.* p. 65 180–193).

75. Cf. Gen 4:3. PetC *Ser* 109 p. 673 39.

76. Typology saw parallels between OT and NT for both evil and good realities. Cain, the first murderer, became regarded as the archetype of various evils. It is not clear why the sacrifice of Cain is deceitful, but this is possibly related to the fact that Cain invited Abel to a quiet place with murderous intent (note his comment at Mark 15:20). The author points to a parallel with the vinegar offered to Jesus (cf. Mark 15:36). Later he will describe this as also deceitful.

77. Greg *Hom* 29 1217 A. The Bible does not say that Joseph was bound, but the selling of Jesus is seen as prefigured in the selling of Joseph (Gen 37:28; cf. Ps 105:17). Gregory makes a similar point (*Forty Gospel Homilies*, p. 231).

78. Ps 105:18. The words may apply to the preceding or following sentence.

79. Arnob. Jnr. *Exp* p. 276 94; Hil *Matt* Mt 26:1, p. 242. John 18:10 names Peter as the one who cuts off the ear. This is seen as an image of his subsequent decision to preach to the gentiles (Acts 10). The early church gradually moved away from preaching to the Jews.

80. Ps 88:18. The ancient commentators saw no difficulty reading such verses in reference to Jesus.

Whoever wants to escape from the hands of wicked people, let them mentally abandon the things of the world, and flee after Jesus.[81]

The priests and the scribes assembled (Mark 14:53).

Then, there takes place *the assembly of the bulls among the cows of the peoples.*[82] Peter follows from a distance. Here is *a man with two minds, inconstant in all his ways.*[83] Fear draws back but love draws forward. He warms himself at the fire in the courtyard with the servants. The courtyard of the priest is the setting of this world; the servants are the demons; the fire stands for carnal desire. Whoever remains with them cannot weep for sins. The high priests were looking for false witness against Jesus. *Iniquity has lied to itself.*[84] This is like the queen accusing Joseph, and the priests accusing Susanna.[85] However, fire without fuel dies out, and *there were no witnesses in agreement* (Mark 14:56). What varies is regarded as uncertain. Some said, *We heard this man saying, "I will destroy this temple"* (Mark 14:58). It is a custom for heretics to extract an imperfect representation from the truth. He did not say what they claim, but a similar expression about the temple of his own body which after three days he reawakened.[86]

The High Priest standing interrogates Jesus, **but he remained silent** (cf. Mark 14:60–61).

Here, *like a sheep to the slaughter* he is led voiceless.[87] *He was dumb and kept silence in regard to good things.*[88] The silence of Christ absolves the excuse of Adam.[89]

And he says to him, "Are you the Christ, the son of the living blessed God?" (Mark 14:61).

---

81. Cf. Gen 39:6–20.
82. Ps 68:38b is used in the tradition to suggest persecution. It is applied to the case of Jesus, though not with great aptness. Eucherius explains that bulls are the leaders of the people, while cows stand for people full of carnal vices (*Form* p. 27 15, 20–21).
83. James 1:8.
84. Ps 27:12.
85. Cf. Gen 39:6–20; the description of Potiphar's wife as a "queen" is incorrect. Cf. Dan 13; the biblical text does not say that the two men were priests.
86. Heretics, he asserts, are like false witnesses. The recurring references to heretics are difficult to assess. Is the author thinking of any in particular, e.g., Arians in his vicinity, or are such comments conventional? The influence of the parallel John 2:19 is discernible in the term "awakened."
87. Cf. Is 53:7.
88. Ps 39:2.
89. Adam tries to talk himself out of trouble in Gen 3:12.

Whom they were expecting in the long term, they do not recognize when he is near. It was the same in the case of Isaac, who with dimmed eyes, does not recognize Jacob under his hands, but sings about the future, far removed from him.[90]

Jesus, however, said to him, "I am" (Mark 14:62).
So that they would be without excuse.[91]

And you will see the Son of Man (Mark 14:62).
The priest interrogates the Son of God but Jesus replies "Son of Man." This was in order that we may understand that the Son of God is the same as the Son of Man, lest we make a quaternity in the Trinity. It is necessary that the man be in the God and the God in the man.[92]

Sitting at the right hand of the power (Mark 14:62).
That is, reigning in eternal life, and in divine power.[93]

And coming on the clouds of heaven (Matt 26:64).[94]
He ascends in a cloud,[95] he will come in a cloud. That is, he ascends only in his body that he took from a virgin, and he will come for judgment with the many-faceted church, *which is his body and its fullness.*[96] As it says, according to Matthew, *Since the Son of Man will come,* and *all his angels with him,* etc.[97]

The High Priest tore his garments. That is the Jews lost the ephod which they used to revere. Here is Samuel and the cloak and the kingdom torn from

90. Greg *Hom* 10 111 C. The High Priest, representing the Jewish people, is faulted for not recognizing the Messiah. Isaac in Gen 27:23 does not recognize Jacob, but in Gen 27:27–29 utters a blessing concerning the future of Jacob's descendants. There is a close parallel in a homily of Gregory the Great (*Forty Gospel Homilies,* p. 56).

91. Rom 1:20.

92. While the High Priest is not faulted for failing to understand the mystery of the Trinity, the interchange provides an occasion for the commentator to clarify matters. The Old Irish Gloss lists the four, Father, Son of God, Son of Man, and Holy Spirit (*Thes. Pal.,* p. 490). The foursome is avoided by the union of humanity and divinity in the person of Christ.

93. The author again explains that the sitting position represents the act of reigning.

94. A parallel version of the phrase in quoted from Matthew.

95. Cf. Acts 1:9.

96. Eph 1:23.

97. Matt 25:31. Matthew adds the detail of "angels," who are understood to be the members of the church in heaven.

the hands of Saul.[98] The gentile soldiers do not tear Christ's tunic,[99] while the priest tears the dignity of his priesthood.

And they condemn him as **guilty of death** (cf. Mark 14:64).[100]

This was so that by his guilt he might remove our guilt; that by the blindfold on his face, he might take the blindfold from our hearts; that by receiving the spits, he might wash the face of our soul; that by the blows, by which he was struck on the head,[101] he might heal the head of the human race, which is Adam; that by the blows by which he was slapped, his greatest praise might applaud by means of our hands and lips; as it is said, *All nations, clap your hands;*[102] that by his cross he might eliminate our torment; that by his death, he might put to death our death. With the shape of a serpent he kills the serpent, because by a serpent produced from a rod the other serpents are swallowed up.[103] For that reason, he himself says through the prophet, *Death, I will be the death of you, and Hell, I will be your bite.*[104] The insults he suffered removed our shame. His bonds made us free.[105] By the crown of thorns on his head,[106] we have obtained the diadem of the kingdom.[107] By his wounds we have been healed.[108] By his burial we resurrect. By his descent into hell we ascend into heaven.[109] This is like finding honey *in the mouth* of the *dead lion.*[110] The prophet foresaw

98. Cf. 1 Sam 15:27–28. There is not a perfect match between the two incidents, but this tradition of commentary was adept at spotting points of resemblance and simply editing out the others.

99. Cf. John 19:23–24.

100. There follows a series of parallels between the details of Jesus' sufferings and death and their efficaciousness for our salvation. Morin saw the influence of Sedulius in this passage ("Un commentaire romain," p. 355). He notes parallels between some of the details and Sedulius's *Carmen Paschale* (V, p. 121 101–103).

101. This detail of the blow on the head is from Mark 15:19.

102. Ps 47:1.

103. The basic principle operating here, the author points out, is the same as that which led Moses to counteract the danger of the serpents in Numbers 21:4–9 and John 3:14. Cf. Ex 7:8–12.

104. Hos 13:14. Greg *Hom* 22 1177 C. Note the logic that allowed the author to speak like this: God spoke through the prophets; Jesus is God; therefore, the words are his. A very similar usage in regard to the same text (Hos 13:14) is found in Gregory: "Hence he [the Lord Jesus] says truly by the mouth of Hosea . . ." (*Forty Gospel Homilies*, p. 169).

105. Cf. Mark 15:1.

106. Cf. Mark 15:17.

107. Cf. Is 62:3.

108. Cf. Is 53:5.

109. Christ's descent is based on an understanding of 1 Pet 3:19. The author referred to the mystery previously.

110. Cf. Judges 14:8. Further parallels with the story of Samson will follow.

all these things and said, *What shall I render to the Lord for all that he has rendered to me?*[111]

And while Peter was in the courtyard, etc. (Mark 14:66).

Peter without the spirit surrendered to the voice of the maidservant; with the Spirit he does not surrender even to princes and kings.[112] The first maidservant represents the titillation, the second is the consent, and the third man is the act itself.[113] The recalling of the word of Christ washes away this triple denial by means of tears. Then, the cock crows for us when any preacher stirs up our hearts to sorrow through repentance. Then, we begin to weep when we are set alight, internally, by the spark of knowledge, and, externally, we go out beyond what we have been.[114]

111. Ps 116:12. The psalmist is pictured as giving thanks in anticipation of the blessings of Christ's redemptive work. This is different from the practice of praying such a psalm in the light of NT revelation. The author suggests that the psalmist saw what was to come.

112. The mention of princes and kings appears to be an allusion to the words of Jesus in Matt 10:18.

113. Peter's denials are allegorized in terms of the stages of temptation.

114. Peter's story is meant to be a model for all. Before, in commenting on Jesus' foretelling of Peter's betrayal, the author mentioned how the Holy Spirit can work through prophecy and the apostles. The mention of knowledge (*scientia*) is possibly an allusion to one of the gifts of the Spirit.

CHAPTER 15

They hand the bound Jesus over to Pilate (cf. Mark 15:1). Here is Samson bound by Delilah. Samson means "their sun," since for them the sun went down at noon. Delilah means "a bucket," which stands for the synagogue, which like a bucket does not keep liquid pure but collects all kinds of unclean rubbish.[1] Our Samson, with the jawbone of his word, strikes down innumerable crowds of Jews and demons here.[2] For us who thirst, who are his body, he opens the fountain of eternal life.[3]

---

1. Jerome *Nom* p. 101 23; p. 157 14–15; p. 99 6. The Jews betray Jesus and hand him over to his enemies in a manner comparable to Delilah's treatment of Samson in Judges 16:18–21. The meaning given for the name Samson allows for an anti-Jewish statement. It is remarkable that in two successive sentences the same OT character has contrary meanings imposed on him. The demands of the author's purpose can sometimes force allegory into this jolting type of maneuver. The name Delilah is also used to attack the Jews (cf. Num 19:15).

2. Judges 15:15–17 recounts how Samson slew the Philistines with the jawbone of the ass. The Turin Gloss (*Thes. Pal.*, p. 492, 1.20) says Samson used the jawbone of a camel. This may be due to confusion with the story, found in the Irish tradition, of Abel being murdered with the jawbone of a camel (e.g., "Adam and His Descendants" [5:11], in Máire Herbert and Martin McNamara, *Irish Biblical Apocrypha* [pp. 18, 167]). "Our Samson" uses his word as a weapon. The use of allegory becomes quite bizarre in this instance, where the image of a Jewish hero killing enemies is used to portray the killing (albeit not literally) of Jews.

3. The transition to a thought close to that of John 4:14 is sudden. Maybe it is intended as a contrast to the bucket of liquid just mentioned.

The High Priests stirred up the crowds so that they would ask for Barabbas, and so that they might crucify Jesus (cf. Mark 15:11). Here we have the two goats.[4] One is termed ἀποπομαῖος meaning "the scapegoat."[5] He is set free with the sin of the people and sent into the desert of hell. The other goat is slain like a lamb for the sins of those who have been set free. The Lord's portion is always slaughtered. The portion of the devil, who is their master, is cast out, without restriction, into the infernal regions.[6]

The soldiers **dress Jesus in purple clothes,** etc. (cf. Mark 15:17).

He is stripped of his own clothes, that is, the Jewish ones, and is clothed in purple, that is, with the church of the gentiles, which has been collected from the rocks of the sea. In due course he is stripped of the purple and, finally, he is dressed again with the scandalous Jewish people. When *the full number of the gentiles* will have come in, *all Israel* will be saved.[7]

And they bring him forward to crucify him (Mark 15:20).[8]

Here Abel is led out into the field by his brother so that he may be slain. Here we have Isaac with wood, and Abraham with the ram caught in the

---

4. Cf. Lev 16:5.
5. Cf. Lev 16:10.
6. Cf. 2 Pet 2:4. The ritual of Lev 16 is used to comment on the choice of Barabbas over Jesus. Barabbas is the scapegoat. Jesus is the goat that is slaughtered. The comparison presents an understanding of the expiatory value of Jesus' death, but the freeing of Barabbas has no real relation to the OT image. The term ἀποπομπαῖος is used in the Greek (LXX) text of Lev 16. The Vulgate translates as *emissarius*. All of the manuscript readings are, to a greater or lesser extent, corrupt. Either the author took over the term from a source incorrectly, or else copyists without Greek erred.

7. The changes of clothes is construed in terms of the Jew-Gentile rejection-acceptance, with the eventual salvation of the Jews. The linking of the gentiles with purple appears to be due to association with the Phoenicians who lived to the northwest of Israel. They owe their name to the manufacture of a purple-red dye from seashells gathered from the rocks. The Turin Gloss explains, incorrectly, that the dye was made from plants found on the rocks (*Thes. Pal.*, p. 492, l.42). Previously, the author took the Syro-Phoenician woman and daughter as representing the gentiles. Rom 11:25d-26a is quoted (inverted) to explain why Jesus is once again dressed in his own (i.e., Jewish) clothes. This eventual salvation of the Jews is a preoccupation of the author.

8. There follows a series of OT prefigurements of Jesus carrying his cross. Typology has been helpfully described as "narrative analogy" (Robert Alter, *The Art of Biblical Narrative*, p. 21). Each image is characterized by some detail, usually wood, which evokes the cross and passion of Christ: Abel (Gen 4:8), Isaac (Gen 22:6), Abraham (Gen 22:13 LXX), Joseph (Gen 37:7), Moses (Ex 17:5), Moses (Num 21:8–9), grapes (Num 13:23–24), Elisha (2 Kings 6:5–7), and Jonah (Jon 1:15; 2:2).

thicket.[9] Here is Joseph with the sheaf he dreamt about,[10] and with his long robe smeared in blood. Here is Moses with the rod and with the serpent suspended on the pole. Here is the bunch of grapes carried on the stick.[11] Here we have Elisha with the wood for getting the axe which had sunk to the bottom; the axe floated up to the wood.[12] This wood represents the human race which fell into hell from the forbidden tree and which, through the wood of the cross of Christ and the baptism of water, floated to paradise. Here is Jonah, because of the wood of the dice, cast into the sea and into the belly of the whale for three days.[13]

And they forced **a certain Simon of Cyrene, the father of Alexander and Rufus, who was passing by, coming from the country,** etc. (cf. Mark 15:21).

Some are remembered because of the merits of their fathers; others because of those of their children. This Simon, however, who was forced to carry the cross, is remembered because of the merits of his sons who were disciples. By this, we, in this present life, are reminded that parents are helped by the wisdom of their offspring. So the Jewish people is remembered because of the merits of patriarchs, prophets and apostles. For from the bitterness of the root springs the sweetness of the olive. For this reason, it is said to Judea through Jeremiah, *The Lord called you a name: a ripe, beautiful, fruitful, fair, olive tree.*[14]

---

9. C. Arles *Ser* 84 p. 346 no. 331.3. The text preserves a corrupt form ("sabeth") of the Hebrew term (*sabech*) for the thicket which held the ram in Gen 22:13. In the Septuagint, the term was both translated and retained, side by side. This is not found in the Vulgate. The Old Latin imitates the LXX usage in preserving the Hebrew term. Insofar as is evidenced by the patristic witnesses cited in the *Vetus Latina*, the same incorrect form "sabeth" is uniquely found in the writings of Eucherius, where it is explained in glossary style as the Hebrew name for "bush" (*Ins* pp. 147–148). This fact, combined with the evidence of the other correspondences noted between the works, suggests with reasonable certainty the Gospel commentator used the work of Eucherius. The fact that the Hebrew term is not found in the Vulgate raises the question as to why the author felt free to simply give the Hebrew term without further explanation. That it was not generally understood is illustrated by the fact that the Old Irish Turin Gloss incorrectly explains it as "on that day" apparently thinking of the "sabbath" (*Thes. Pal.*, p. 493, l.19).

10. PsHil *Iac* p. 67 523–524.

11. Euch *Form* p. 16 19.

12. C. Arles *Ser* 112 p. 464 no. 444.4.

13. The reference to Jonah points to the last act of the passion, the burial and descent into the underworld.

14. A general moral is drawn from the mention of Simon, and then it is given a special application to the Jewish people. Given the frequent harsh criticism of the Jews in the commentary, it is essential to take note of the positive evaluations when they occur. Nu-

To carry his cross (Mark 15:21).

Just as they used to read, "Cursed be everyone *who hangs on a tree*," he was accursed that he might bear the curse.[15] Simon, who carries the cross because he is forced to, stands for the type who works for human praise.[16] Men force him to perform this task, whom the fear and love of God do not.[17]

What does the very shape of the cross represent if not the fourfold form of the world? The East "shines from the top"; "North holds the right"; South stands on the left; West is secured underfoot.[18] For this reason, the Apostle also says, *That we may know the height, the width, the length, and the depth.*[19] Birds when they fly up in the sky assume the shape of a cross. A human person adopts the shape of a cross when swimming in water, or when praying. A ship crossing the seas is blown along by a mast shaped like a cross. The letter "T" is described as a sign of salvation and of the cross.[20]

---

anced and begrudging though it may be, here is acknowledgment of the OT and NT Jews, offspring of the Jewish people, who were called by God to save the world. Jer 11:16 is quoted to round off the compliment.

15. Cf. Deut 21:23 (Gal 3:13a).

16. Greg *Hom* 32 1234 D.

17. Cf. Gregory the Great, *Forty Gospel Homilies*, p. 260.

18. The sequence in which the cardinal points are listed would seem to be of importance for providing a clue to origins. Previously, directions had a cultural and religious significance. The eastern orientation of the Jerusalem Temple and, later, of church buildings gave priority to that direction in the Jewish-Christian tradition, though this was not universal. The author lists ENSW. At Mark 12:1, the author has EWSN, though his source text, Luke 13:29, has EWNS. The variables make it difficult to get an exact cultural and historical fit for the sequence found in the commentary. Morin ("Un commentaire romain," p. 354) proposed parallels between the commentary text here and Sedulius's *Carmen Paschale* (V, pp. 128–129, 188–195). I recognize the parallels (as the quotation marks indicate), but in the matter of orientation, the sequence of Sedulius is EWNS. This orientation is found in "The Vision of Adomnán," but on the next page we find EWSN, though the idiom here is different (Máire Herbert and Martin McNamara, *Irish Biblical Apocrypha*, pp. 138, no. 4, and p. 139, no. 11).

Another complication arises when we consider that the author is looking at the cross, so that we might have a mirror image of how he recites the sequence.

There is an Irish text in *The Stowe Missal* (ed. George F. Warner) which shows an awareness of the difference that arises from one's perspective: "arissíar robui aiged crist in cruce id est contra civitatem isair robúi aigeth longini arrothuaisre dosuidui issed ropodesse do crist" (p. 38). This is translated as: "For westwards was Christ's face on the Cross, to wit, contra civitatem, and eastwards was the face of Longinus; what to him was left, to Christ was the right" (p. 41).

19. The four dimensions of the cross are matched in this amalgam and accommodation of Eph 3:18 and Rom 8:39.

20. Greg *Iob* 30.25 p. 1542 119–120. Cf. Ez 9:4–6. The author finds reminders of the shape of the cross in nature and human activity. The custom of praying with outstretched arms is attested in Ireland, but not exclusively.

And they brought him to Golgotha, which means "Calvary" (cf. Mark 15:22).

The Jews have a tradition that on this very mountain, the ram was sacrificed for Isaac.[21] There he is beheaded, that is to say, Christ is separated from his own flesh, namely from physical Judaism.

And they gave him wine mixed with myrrh to drink (Mark 15:23).

By means of this wine-vinegar the deadly apple juice is counteracted.[22]

And he did not accept (Mark 15:23), that is to say, anything for which he suffers. For this reason, it is said about him, *I was repaying what I did not rob.*[23]

And they crucify him (cf. Mark 15:25). To this tree salvation is transfixed; death was impaled on the first tree. The first tree is the tree of the knowledge of good and evil. The second tree is for us the tree of good alone, and is the tree of life.[24] The first hand reached out to the tree and grasped death; the second hand reached out and discovered the life that had been lost.[25] On this tree we are carried through the surging sea to *the land of the living.*[26]

---

21. The author's assertion is puzzling. He appears to confuse two traditions, one to do with Moriah and one to do with Calvary. In the original Hebrew of Gen 22:2, Abraham is told to go to "the land of Moriah" to sacrifice Isaac. The Greek and Latin translations did not preserve the place-name, but used translations based on etymologies. 2 Chron 3:1 names the site of Solomon's temple as "Moriah," but without any explicit reference to Abraham's sacrifice. The author refers to a Jewish tradition. But such a tradition about Moriah is certainly very different from any to do with Calvary, which Christian tradition invested with many legends involving OT times, even back to Adam. Calvary is never identified with the Moriah of Solomon's temple by Christians and, a fortiori, most certainly not by Jews.

The detail of "beheading" in the commentary text appears to depend on Jerome (followed by Eucherius), who argues that criminals used to be beheaded on that spot (Jerome *Math* p. 270 1679–1685; Euch *Ins* p. 152 18–20).

22. We have here an allusion to the fruit of Gen 3:6, popularly taken to be an apple.

23. Ps 69:4c is quoted as a commentary on the refusal of Jesus. The suffering of Jesus, which he did not wish to evade, was entirely for the sake of others. The author plays on the sense of "take"; Jesus did not take anything for which he should be punished.

24. He contrasts the salvation brought about by the cross (the second tree) and the death caused by the tree in Eden. The ambiguity of the first tree (Gen 2:9) is resolved by the second tree. The two trees of Gen 2:9 are alluded to.

25. The spread of Jesus' hands on the cross evokes a contrast with Eve's reaching for the fruit. God excluded Adam and Eve from Eden lest they reach for the fruit of the tree of life (cf. Gen 3:22), but now Jesus' crucifixion ensures life.

26. Cf. Ps 27:13.

And they divided [his] **garments,** etc. (cf. Mark 15:24).

The garments of the Lord are his commandments,[27] which cover his body, *which is the church.*[28] These are divided among the gentile soldiers so that there may be four groups with one faith: the married, the widowed, those in charge, and those set apart.[29] The undivided cloak is gambled for, representing peace and unity without seam, like a royal signet ring.[30]

Now it was the third hour and they crucified him (Mark 15:25).

Indeed it is only Mark who has provided this detail. For at the sixth hour darkness covered the earth, so that no one could wag the head.[31] For in Mark's account the harvest goes from 30-fold up to 100-fold, that is, from the third hour of the cross up to the third day of the resurrection. The 30-fold harvest is found on the cross, the 60-fold in the underworld, and the 100-fold in paradise.[32]

And the title of the charge against him was written above, "The King of the Jews" (Mark 15:26).

As is prefaced in the Psalm titles, *To the end. Do not destroy.*[33] The notice is in three languages: "*malchus* of the Jews, *basilius exomologesson*, king of confessors." This means "King of the Jews" in Hebrew and "King of confessors" in Greek and Latin. These three languages have been consecrated to dominance

27. Jerome *Math* p. 126 1394.
28. Col 1:24.
29. The soldiers are numbered as four in John 19:23. The basis of division is not clear so that the translation must remain conjectural. It is normal in the literature to find the faithful divided into groups. The basis for division varies. Bischoff notes, in the case of another work he identifies as Irish, a commentary on John's Gospel, that the garments are allotted to "single, joined, ruler and subject," where the language is close to our text: "four groups: the separated, the joined, the one in charge and the subject, or the four parts of the world" (*quottuor ordines, id est separatus et coniunctus, praepositus et subiectus vel quottuor mundi partes*) ("Turning-Points," p. 137).
30. Cf. John 19:23–24. The undivided cloak is found only in John. The gambling is reserved for the cloak in John's account, whereas the Synoptics have it for the garments.
31. The idiom "wagging the head" is used in Mark 15:29 to describe the mocking behavior of the spectators. The darkness shields Jesus from this disrespect.
32. The author notes the time given as proper to Mark and sees a tie with the third day of resurrection. He also links it to the mention of the sixth hour in Mark 15:33 as part of an allegory, with the varying yields in the parable of the sower (cf. Mark 4:8). The crescendo is proper to Mark.
33. The Psalm titles are referred to as a category. The ancient commentators regarded them as part of Sacred Scripture. This is the Vulgate version of the title to Ps 75. Here it appears to be used to identify the psalm with features that link it with this part of the passion account, e.g., the mention of the Lord holding the cup of wine.

in the title on the cross of Christ, so that every language may record the treachery of the Jews.[34]

And with him **two robbers,** etc. (cf. Mark 15:27).

Truth was classified among the wicked.[35] He abandoned the one on the left, but he raises up the one on the right.[36] Just as he does on the day of judgment; for the similar crime, a dissimilar life is their lot! One precedes Peter into heaven, while the other precedes Judas into hell. A brief confession acquired a long life, while a single blasphemy is punished with an eternal penalty.

Here is Judah's colt tied to the vine.[37] Here is the ἀναβολαίον, that is, the garment dyed in the blood of the grape.[38] Here the goats tear at the vine, blaspheming him and *wagging their heads* (Mark 15:29).[39] The death is put upon the

34. John 19:20 supplies the information about the three languages. All the manuscripts present the Hebrew form of the title in a corrupt form. *Malchus* is a Latinized version of *melek*, the Hebrew for "king." The Hebrew word for "Jews" is simply translated into Latin. The author correctly notes that the Greek and Latin forms of the notice say something different from that of the Hebrew. The traditional etymology of *Judaei* is "those who confess," and this explains the translations of the Greek and Latin (Jerome *Nom* p. 67 19; p. 152 15; p. 154 22; p. 157 4; *Dan* p. 863 94–95; Euch *Ins* p. 103 1–5; p. 144 13–14). Neither Hebrew nor Greek script is found in any manuscript.

These languages are given an eminent holy status. The idea is found in other writings going back to Jerome. A special interest shown in the three sacred languages is said to be characteristic of Hiberno-Latin biblical commentary (M. Walsh and D. Ó Cróinín, *Cummian's Letter*, pp. 57–59).

35. The OT quotation in Mark 15:28 appears to refer to Is 53:12. In the Lichfield (St. Chad) text of Mark, we read *veritas deputata* (Wordsworth and White, *Novum Testamentum*, p. 264). It is possible that this is meant to be a citation and not a comment on the text. The Lichfield text is regarded as a major witness to the Celtic tradition of the biblical text. The Lichfield text is now dated to the second half of the eighth century. (See Martin McNamara, *Studies on Texts of Early Irish Latin Gospels*, p. 21.)

36. Cf. Luke 23:39–43. The fate of those on right and left corresponds to that of the judgment parable in Matt 25:31–46.

37. Cf. Gen 49:11.

38. Cf. Gen 49:11. The Greek term used is puzzling. In the Septuagint Greek of Gen 49:11b, *peribolēn* is used. Liddell and Scott list *anabolaion* as a diminutive of *anabolē* and note its use by Symmachus (an early Greek translator used by Origen in his *Hexapla*) in Is 3:22. How it turns up here is difficult to explain. It suggests the use of a source which quickly became unintelligible to copyists.

39. There are similar elements to be noted in Gen 40:9 and 19, but the link is tenuous. Jewish legend pictured a goat eating from Noah's vine, and a parallel with Noah's drunken stupor is proposed soon (see Don Cameron Allen, *The Legend of Noah*, p. 116, n. 14; p. 173, n. 139). However, the most likely source is a legend recounted by Hyginus (a lesser-known contemporary of Ovid): the gods give Hyginus the gift of a vine, but it is damaged by a goat. A version of this story is found in a poem by the Anglo-Saxon writer Aldhelmus (639–709); see his "De Virginitate" (Carmen), *Aldhelmi Opera*, p. 468, lines 2845–2846. Another version is found in an anthology dating from the seventh or eighth century known

heads of the wicked, when the chains of hell are shaken, even to the neck of Adam, who is the neck of the human race.[40]

Come down from the cross (Matt 27:40).[41]

Lest he accomplish the salvation which he is beginning![42] Here is a case of *All have turned aside, altogether they have become useless.*[43]

At the sixth hour darkness covered the whole earth (Mark 15:33).

Here is Noah, drunk and naked, covered by earth and sky as with a dark garment, and mocked by mankind.[44] Here blood dripped *from the wood.*[45]

At the ninth hour, Jesus shouted with a loud cry, "Heloy, heloy, lama sabacthani," that is, "my God, my God, why have you abandoned me?" (Mark 15:34).

This psalm, then, is written *for morning recital,* referring to the morning when Christ was led to the cross.[46] These are the very words of the Son of Man. For this reason, according to Luke, he continues, *Into your hands I commend my spirit.*[47]

---

as *Mythographi Vaticani* (no. 79, pp. 155–156). The legend can be read in the translation of Mary Grant (*The Myths of Hyginus*, p.185). Ps 80:13 may have been in the mind of the expositor.

40. The word "heads" acts a catchword. The author may mean the death of Christ along the lines of the retribution involved in Matt 27:25.

41. This text is not in Mark.

42. I understand and translate the comment as ironic.

43. Ps 14:3a (= Ps 53:3a = Rom 3:12a).

44. Cf. Gen 9:20–23. The modern reader will probably find it hard to relate Jesus in agony to the drunken Noah. This an example of where the typing of OT characters and incidents with the NT story strains our tolerance and our capacity to absorb. The medieval mind was able to concentrate on the commonality and ignore the incongruities of the proposed parallel. Both are not fully conscious; both are naked; both are covered; both are mocked. The biblical text gives no indication that Ham had mocked his father, but this became a standard feature of later medieval exposition. For example, see *The Bible of the Poor (Biblia Pauperum)* (ed. Labriola and Smeltz, pp. 37, 79, 122, 166–167).

45. Cf. IV (= II) Ezra 5:5. Charles Wright notes that the application of the motif of the bleeding tree to the crucifixion is rare ("Hiberno-Latin and Irish-Influenced Biblical Commentaries, Florilegia, and Homily Collections," p. 107).

46. Cf. Mark 15:34, citing Ps 22:1. The Psalm is identified by reference to its title in the Vulgate version. This is very different in the modern translations made from the Hebrew. Many details of this Psalm are quoted in the NT in relation to the passion and death of Jesus. Patristic commentary followed this lead. The mention of morning provides an opportunity.

47. Ps 31:6 as given in Luke 23:46.

At the ninth hour, having swept out the house, the tenth coin which had been lost is found.[48]

One of them runs and finds a sponge, something just like themselves, empty, weak, dried up, fit for the fire.[49] He fills it with vinegar, that is with wickedness and deceit. About this it is said, "*I planted you as a vine* of Sorech, and how is it that *you have changed to* the bitterness of a unknown vine"; and "*I expected that it would produce grapes*, but it produced thorns."[50]

Jesus gave a loud cry and died (Mark 15:37).

And indeed, the flesh was weakened but the divine voice grew strong. It said, *Open to me the doors of righteousness. I will go in and acknowledge the Lord.*[51] We die with a low cry or without any, because we are of the earth. However, he dies with a raised cry because he has come down from heaven. *The veil of the temple* is torn (cf. Mark 15:38), that is to say, heaven is opened.[52]

The centurion says, *Truly*, he was *the Son of God* (cf. Mark 15:39). Now are the *last* made *first*.[53] The gentile people confesses; the blind Jewish people denies, so that *an error worse than the previous one* happens to them.[54]

There were also women watching from a distance, etc. (Mark 15:40).

Just as the Virgin Mary ensures that the feminine sex is not excluded from salvation, so indeed the widow Mary Magdalene and the other mothers ensure

---

48. The number nine calls to mind the woman with nine coins (Luke 15:8–10). Her finding of the missing tenth is the parable's way of expressing the salvation of the lost sinner.

49. Euch *Form* p. 47 1.

50. At Mark 14:43, this incident is mentioned with the same association of vinegar and deceit. Vinegar looks like wine, but its appearance deceives. God is pictured as deceived in Is 5:4 and Jer 2:21. *Sorech* represents the Hebrew word used in the Hebrew text of both Jer 2:21 and Is 5:2, the two texts quoted in an accommodated form. *Sorech* is preserved in the LXX Greek of Isaiah but not in the case of Jeremiah. This is the opposite of what we find in the Latin text of the commentary, where the Hebrew *Sorech* is found in the text from Jeremiah. The Vulgate does not use the Hebrew term in either text. It is possible that an Old Latin version has influenced the forms of the quotations, though I have not been able to identify a perfect match.

51. Ps 118:19.

52. Cf. Heb 9:24.

53. Cf. Mark 10:31.

54. Cf. Matt 27:64.

that it is not dissociated from the knowledge of the mystery of the cross and resurrection.[55]

Joseph comes late on the Preparation Day. He was from Arimathea which means "the one who lays down."[56] He comes to lay the body in the tomb. He was *a noble member of the Council* and he was looking for *the kingdom of God* (cf. Mark 15:43). He approaches Pilate and asks for the body of Jesus. He buys a linen cloth. He wraps the body in it and places it *in the tomb, which had been cut out of the rock* (Mark 15:46). He rolls a boulder to the mouth of the tomb. The Marys watch where he was laid (cf. Mark 15:47).

All of this corresponds to the Jewish people who finally believe.[57] They are ennobled in faith to become children of Abraham. They lay to rest despair, and *look for the kingdom of God* (cf. Mark 15:43). They approach Christians to be baptized. What does the name of Pilate mean? It means "Hammer-man,"[58] that is, he who subdues the ironlike gentiles, so that he might rule them with *a rod of iron*.[59] The Jewish people asks for the sacrifice which is granted to penitents at the end as a viaticum.[60] And with a clean heart dead to sins, they wrap

55. Greg *Hom* 3 1086 C; 12 1119 A. Gregory makes similar points about the involvement of the two sexes ("Both sexes are gathered into the faith," *Forty Gospel Homilies*, p. 5; "the entire number of faithful is gathered in from the two sexes," p. 69). This is the first record of the labeling of Mary Magdalene as a widow (see G. Morin, "Un traité inédit d'Arnobe le Jeune," p. 159, n. 2). Morin compares the title "widow" used in the commentary with Arnobius's description of Mary Magdalene as a "matron." Mary Magdalene was to become the subject of extravagant legend in the Latin West.

56. Jerome *Nom* p. 114 12–13 (*deiciens*). The explanation of "Arimathea" is somewhat different from that proposed by Jerome, while Eucherius is silent.

57. The Gospel text has been summarized, and the details will now be allegorized. The actions of Joseph are understood as a portrayal of the destiny of the Jews. Despite his harsh criticism of the Jews, the author never considers them lost and damned. As Joseph was noble, they will be ennobled through faith to become children of Abraham, the model for Christian faith.

58. Cf. Jerome *Nom* p. 141 18–19; cf. Euch *Ins* p. 144 11. Both have *os malleatoris* which is not the same as *nomen Pilati, id est malleatoris* in the commentary text.

59. As "Arimathea" means "laying aside," they will lay aside despair; as he looked for the kingdom of God, so will the Jews. As Joseph approached Pilate, so will the Jews approach the gentile Christians. Pilate, who was a gentile, is given another identity by linking the meaning of his name, "hammer," with iron (cf. Gen 4:22). This is associated with the picture of God ruling the gentiles with rod of iron (Ps 2:9; Rev 2:7; 12:5; 19:5). The result is that Pilate stands for God.

60. As Joseph asks for the body of Jesus, so will the Jews seek and be given his eucharistic body as viaticum.

in the defense of faith, that which was made firm with the covering of hope, and they bring it to conclusion through works of charity. Indeed, *the purpose of the law is love*[61] for the chosen ones who are watching from afar, who are like "the drops in the sea."[62] This will take place when, *if that were possible, even the chosen ones* will be led astray.[63]

61. 1 Tim 1:5.

62. The three Marys are described as watching from a distance in Mark 15:40, 47. I understand the Marys to represent the far-off gentiles. They will be the ones that the Jews will one day approach. The inclusion of the gentiles in the allegory conforms to the general interest in the commentary in the Jew-Gentile issue. Throughout the commentary, the Jews are near or within, while the gentiles are far away or without. As we have already seen from other examples in the commentary, the fact that the women are Jewish does not prevent them from having an allegorical meaning of gentiles.

Did the author write *stillae* ("drops") or *stellae* ("stars")? The evidence favors *stillae*. The explanation of the name "Mary" as "star of the sea" became part of Marian devotion. The same problem of scribal confusion arises in the case of the meaning proposed by Jerome. The critical edition opts for *stilla maris* (*Nom* p. 76 8).

63. Cf. Matt 24:10, 24; cf. Mark 13:22. The text appears to have been suggested by the words "chosen ones," and it evokes the end times, when the Jews will find faith.

CHAPTER 16

When the sabbath had ended, etc., as far as the end (Mark 16:1).[1]

We will now sprinkle our book, and the compartment of our mind,[2] with scent-giving spices, in union with the bride and the young folk who run after her.[3] Now the King brings us into his chambers.[4] Now, Mary the beloved, rises up.[5] Winter is over and the rain has stopped,[6] flowers have been seen in the land, *the cooing of the dove has been heard in our land,*[7] the blossoming vines *have given out fragrance.*[8] The bridegroom returns from the shadow in which he sleeps *at midday.*[9] "After the sad sabbath" a happy day shines forth. This is the most important of days, since as first light dawns on that important day,[10] my Lord rises up in triumph, and says, *This is the day the Lord has made; let us rejoice and be glad in it.*[11]

1. The author denotes the whole section dealing with the resurrection. He ushers in a new section by sprinkling the book with "spices" (a term occurring in Mark 16:1), just as he opened the beginning of the passion account with a sprinkling with blood.
2. PasR *Math* p. 372 358.
3. Cf. Song 1:2–3.
4. Cf. Song 2:4.
5. Cf. Song 2:11–13.
6. Cf. Song 2:11.
7. Song 2:12.
8. Cf. Song 2:13.
9. Cf. Song 1:17.
10. Sed *Car* V p. 137 315–316.
11. Ps 118:24 is quoted according to the Mozarabic text (i.e., more accurately, the Visigothic tradition of Old Latin, which developed in Spain). There is probably an echo to

And very early, when the sun was up, on the first day of the week, they come to the tomb (Mark 16:2).

The true sun rises after the setting of the body. Here the eagles gather around the body,[12] as the mothers and the apostles see the boulder rolled aside, namely, the law of death,[13] as if it were to say, *Death, where is your sting?* etc.[14]

For it was very big (Mark 16:4).

It touches even infants in the womb. It is the complaint of all and weighs on everyone.[15]

And entering the tomb, they saw a young man (Mark 16:5).

Not an old man, not a child, but someone of the delightful age. As it is said, *Rejoice, young person, in your youth.*[16] True youth is not found here, tainted as it is with decay.[17]

Sitting on the right (Mark 16:5).

That is, reigning in good fortune.[18] This youth displays the appearance of the resurrection to those who fear death.

Clothed in a white gown (Mark 16:5).

This stands for true joy, now that the enemy has been repelled, and the kingdom has been obtained. The king of peace has been sought and found, and never abandoned.

They were astonished (Mark 16:5).

That is *because eye has not seen, nor ear has heard, nor has it entered into the heart of man, what God has prepared* for those who love him.[19]

---

be noted of Ps 110:1, *Domino meo* ("to my Lord"), as this Psalm was read in reference to Christ's glorification.

12. Cf. Matt 24:28.

13. Cf. Rom 8:2.

14. 1 Cor 15:55b.

15. This is one of the most striking examples of the reach of the allegorical method. A Scripture text, which follows upon an already established allegory, is recognized as having the potential for sustaining the allegory and is swallowed up into its mechanism.

16. Eccles 11:9.

17. The fact that the text specifies a youth is regarded as having significance. The negative view of this world, which permeates the commentary, is reinforced by the stress on the transitory nature of youthfulness.

18. "Sitting" is once again glossed as "reigning."

19. Cf. 1 Cor 2:9.

Who said to them, "Do not be afraid" (Mark 16:6).

God is love.[20] Therefore, *there is no fear in God's love.*[21] What should they fear, they who have found the one they sought?[22]

You are looking for Jesus the Nazarene.

The bitter root of the cross has vanished, and the blossom of life has burst forth with fruit, that is, what was laid low in death has risen in glory.

Look, there is the place.

It is shown to mortals in order to elicit due thanksgiving. This is so that we may understand what we were, and that we might know what we will be.

But go and tell (Mark 16:7).

The women are told to inform the apostles. Because death was announced through a woman, so through a woman, the news of resurrection life.[23]

To Peter

This is the man who considers himself unfit for discipleship, since he denied the master three times. Past sins do not harm when they do not please.[24]

He has gone ahead to Galilee.

There are gathered *the scattered of Israel*, and there are healed *the brokenhearted.*[25]

There you will see him

But not as you have seen him.

But they went out and fled (Mark 16:8).

This refers to the future life. *And sorrow and groaning will flee.* Before the resurrection of all, the women portray what they do after the resurrection— they flee death and terror.[26]

20. 1 John 4:8.
21. Cf. 1 John 4:18.
22. The author, as is his custom, comments by quoting apt texts, in this case, 1 John 4:8b and 18a. His remark is somewhat forced since the women have not yet found Jesus, but the author understands them to have seen the signs.
23. Cf. Gen 3:17–18. Greg *Hom* 25 1194 A.
24. C. Arles *Ser* 56 p. 249 no. 239; 154 p. 630 no. 596. The denials of Peter are linked with Luke 5:8.
25. Cf. Ps 147:2b–3a.
26. The verb "to flee," used transitively and intransitively, is the link between the statements. Is 35:10 is quoted to express a feature of the eschatological era, when sorrow will be

And they said nothing to anyone.

Because they alone see the mystery of the resurrection who themselves have deserved to see it. John's account goes on to say that Peter got up and ran to the tomb so that he might see for himself what he had heard.[27]

Jesus rose early on the first day of the week (Mark 16:9).[28]

He is revealed first to Mary Magdalene out of whom he had cast *seven devils* (cf. Mark 16:9). This is because the prostitutes and tax collectors enter *the kingdom of God* before the synagogue,[29] just as the robber preceded the apostles.[30]

They weep and mourn because they have not yet seen, but, before long, they will be consoled. *Blessed are they who mourn* now, *because they will be consoled.*[31]

And they, hearing, did not believe (Mark 16:11).

For faith functions here, producing the active life; there, untroubled contemplative vision rules. Here we look at the image *in a mirror*; there we will see truth as it is, *face to face.*[32]

For this reason, it continues: **After these things to two of them walking,** that is, making an effort, **he was shown in another form** (Mark 16:12).

When they told of it, they were not believed. That they saw, like Moses, was not sufficient for the others.[33] Just as Moses says, *Show yourself to me.*[34] Forgetting that he is in the flesh, he demands in this life what we are hoping for, after it in the future.[35]

---

no more. The women flee death since they were just described as typifying the resurrection faith of the church.

27. Cf. John 20:1–10. The author points to a different version of the story, in which someone is told.

28. The author passes over, without comment, to what we today call "the longer ending" of the Gospel.

29. Cf. Matt 21:31.

30. Cf. Luke 23:43.

31. Matt 5:5.

32. Underlying this reflection is the pattern of seeing and believing in John 20:29, along with the paraphrase of 1 Cor 13:12. However, the contrast is found widely in the writings of such as Gregory the Great (e.g., *Ez* 1 5 p. 63 208–211; cf. 1 3 p. 41 265–568).

33. Cf. Ex 3:18.

34. Cf. Ex 33:18.

35. There is an inconsistency in the parallel posited with the story of Moses (cf. Ex 3:18; 33:18). On the one hand, it is used to support the claim of those who saw. On the other hand, it is used to rebuke those who demanded to see.

Finally, he appeared to the eleven of them as they were at table (Mark 16:14).

This was so that all witnesses might recount to everyone what they all saw and heard. He reproves them for not believing, in order that belief may follow. He reproves the hardness of their *stony heart* so that it may be replaced with *a heart of flesh*, full of love.[36]

And he said, "Go into the whole world and preach" (cf. Mark 16:15).

Now, after the Spirit was received, just like clay pots strengthened through fire.[37]

To every creature (Mark 16:15).

That is, they are ordered to preach to the entire human race which has in itself something in common with every created reality, that is, angels, flocks, trees, stones, fire and water, heat and cold, wetness and dryness. Because the human being is said to be the world on a small scale.[38]

Whoever will believe, will be saved; *whoever will not believe will be condemned* (cf. Mark 16:16).

The signs [will follow] **those who will believe** (Mark 16:17).

Mark recounts these signs of believers in the 233d section, corresponding to Matthew and Luke.[39] Whoever wishes to read will do so.

The End. Amen.

---

36. Cf. Ezek 36:26.

37. Acts 2:3 links the Holy Spirit with fire.

38. "Creature" presented a problem for the commentator, as it seemed to suggest preaching to inanimate creation. He uses a familiar idea, namely, that the human being represented the apex of creation, and included elements of all other beings—a microcosm. Gregory the Great uses the same idea in a homily on the same text (*Hom* 29 1214 B; *Forty Gospel Homilies*, p. 227). I have noted similar thinking in Irish texts. For example: "For every substance, every element, and every essence visible in the world were all bound together in the body in which Christ arose, that is, in the body of every human. . . . All the world rose with him because the essence of all the elements was in the body which Jesus assumed" ("The Evernew Tongue," no. 11–13, in *Irish Biblical Apocrypha*, ed. M. Herbert and M. McNamara). See also *Catechesis Celtica*: Adam is described as made of various substances: clay, salt, fire, etc. (p. 111 4–8).

39. Just as he mentioned the Eusebian sections in the prologue, now he brings his commentary to a conclusion by identifying the final section (233d) of Mark's Gospel. The second canon table lists this section as paralleled in Matthew and Luke.

EPILOGUE

In this rapid and sketchy treatment of the Evangelist Mark,[1] I have sprinkled you, my children, with the ashes of the red cow burned in the valley.[2] The red cow represents the flesh of the Lord running with blood.[3] It is he who is addressed in the words: *Who is this who comes up from Edom with stained clothing?*[4] Its ashes are the least of the commandments, which are the little strokes and crumbs which fall from the table of the scribes and pharisees.[5] The valley stands for the humility of Christ. The fire is the pain suffered, by which *he carried our pains.*[6] The water mixed with blood is the chalice of the New Testament. The hyssop is the cross. The scarlet stands for the love with which the Father has loved us.[7] He did not spare his own son.[8] I have sprinkled you with some of these things so that you may become *whiter than snow,*[9] and so that you may be transfigured on the mountain and gleam like snow.[10]

1. The Angers Manuscript appends a formal epilogue.
2. At the beginning of the commentary on Mark 14, he referred to the ritual of the red cow in Num 19. In this passage he allegorizes the details.
3. The expiatory sacrifice of the cow is a type of the sacrificial death of Jesus, whose blood was shed.
4. Is 63:1.
5. The "least commandments" of Matt 5:19 are explained as the "tittles" of Matt 5:18, which are quaintly combined with the crumbs in Mark 7:28 (an image he used in the prologue). These are like the ashes because both are treated with meticulous care. The significance of the ash here is not the same as that of the sprinkled ash of the opening sentence.
6. Cf. Is 53:4; I have translated both instances of the Latin *dolor* as "pain(s)."
7. Cf. Eph 2:4.
8. Cf. Rom 8:32.
9. Cf. Ps 51:7; cf. Is 1:18.
10. Cf. Mark 9:1–2.

APPENDIX

An Interpolated Homily

The beginning of the homily about the seven men who all had her as wife and who did not have a child (cf. Mark 12:18–27).[1]

The sterile woman finally died without having a child by any of the seven brothers. What else can this mean except that the Jewish synagogue has been abandoned, as if dead, by the sevenfold Spirit who filled the seven patriarchs?[2] They did not leave to the synagogue the descendant of Abraham, who is Jesus Christ. Although a child *has been born* to them, nevertheless he is given *to us* who are gentiles.[3] This woman was dead to Christ. At the resurrection she will not be married to any of the seven patriarchs. For the number seven represents

---

1. This passage is an interpolation. It is found in all the manuscripts and was the first of many passages added to the original text. Most of the others are from Cassiodorus, and these texts are readily available. Since it has never been translated, I supply it as an appendix. It is an interesting example of early medieval homiletics. Structured in a series of seven applications of seven, it is a highly ornate composition, which is not matched in the commentary. For a fuller discussion, see my paper "The Identification of an Interpolated Homily in an Early Commentary on Mark."

2. *Cam* 4r 20–4v 26; PsAl *Sept* 1170 A–B; PsBed *Coll* 553 B–C; *Crac* 15 pp. 102–103 130–157. See James Cross, *Cambridge Pembroke College MS. 25*, p. 19, n. 2. The Holy Spirit is sevenfold because of the traditional enumeration of seven gifts.

3. There is a delicious paradox in the allusion to Is 9:6. The synagogue is sterile, but yet Jesus is a son of Abraham. Because he was rejected by the Jews and claimed by the gentiles, de facto sterility was maintained. The Jewish people are considered to be cut off from their own patriarchs, who are presented as sharing in the resurrection.

the totality of perfections. It is the reverse of what Isaiah says, *Seven women will take hold of the one man.*[4]

These are the seven churches which the Lord loves, rebukes, punishes and which worship him in the one faith.[5] These are the seven baskets full of pieces of bread. The loaves are the words of the Holy Spirit. Indeed the baskets are the churches.[6] These breads Jesus blesses and breaks and his disciples distribute to the crowd (cf. Mark 6:41; 8:6).[7]

On the seventh day, he blessed all his works and rested in them.[8] Thus, light was made on the first day, representing *wisdom*; the firmament was made on the second, representing *understanding*; on the third day, dry land representing *counsel*; on the fourth day the luminaries are lighted, representing the *powers*; the birds and fish are made on the fifth day, representing the Spirit's *knowledge*; on the sixth day, living beings, and a living soul that is man made in the image of God, representing *piety*; on the seventh day is made the spirit of *reverential fear* of the Lord, who remains holy forever,[9] and fills *the whole earth.*[10] The holy church is filled, not having *spot* nor *wrinkle.*[11] Why is the sevenfold (i.e., perfect) church filled with reverential fear? Because the righteous person will scarcely be saved.[12] This is the one who begs, *Do not enter into judgment with your servant, Lord, since no living being is righteous in your sight.*[13]

The Holy Spirit sang the Psalter concerning the following seven qualities, recalling[14]: what our carelessness will beget; what our diligence will seek; what divine providence will arrange; what the incitement of an enemy will embezzle;

---

4. Is 4:1.

5. Cf. Rev 1–3. V. Pet *Fab* no. 8. p. 7.

6. Aug *Quaest* p. 131 215–217.

7. There are both similarities and dissimilarities between the allegory here and the one in the commentary on Mark 8:1–10. The commentator explains the baskets as the churches, and he compares the seven loaves to the seven gifts of the Spirit, whereas here the breads are said to be the words of the Spirit.

8. Cf. Gen 2:2. There follows a linkup between the list of gifts in Is 11:2 and the seven days of creation (Gen 1:1–2:4). While the parallels are not always exact, there is a clear dependence here on the treatment of the creation account in Victorinus of Petau (*Fab* no. 7, pp. 6–7). The list Christian tradition terms the seven gifts of the Holy Spirit is based on the Vulgate text of Is 11:2, which lists the extra "piety." Here the term *virtutes* ("powers") replaces *fortitudo* ("fortitude") of the Vulgate text because of the source being followed.

9. Cf. Ps 19:9.

10. Cf. Wis 1:7.

11. Cf. Eph 5:27.

12. Cf. 1 Pet 4:18.

13. Ps 143:2.

14. There is a fresh development here. There is no apparent connection with the seven gifts. Seven states or conditions are listed and will be followed by the Psalter texts from which they are derived. I have not been able to establish the rationale of the list. We have left behind the Gospel text that has merely contributed the number seven to this development.

what slippery forgetfulness will subtract; what human fragility will inflict; what improvident ignorance will conceal. We find all these seven qualities expressed in the psalms, as follows[15]:

1. *He conceived sorrow and brought forth iniquity.*[16]
2. *I have come early and called out.*[17]
3. *You have shown me the unclear and hidden things of your wisdom.*[18]
4. *My enemies have surrounded my soul.*[19]
5. *I have been forgotten like one dead from the heart.*[20]
6. *Since my loins are full of illusions.*[21]
7. *The crimes of my youth and my mistakes, do not remember, Lord.*[22]

The sevenfold spirit purifies and illuminates these states,[23] just as the seven lamps shining from the south drive away the northern darknesses of the tabernacle of the covenant.[24] The spirit of wisdom quickly drives away carelessness. The spirit of understanding rationally seeks for diligence. The spirit of counsel prudently finds divine providence. The spirit of power bravely resists incitements. The spirit of knowledge does not allow slippery forgetfulness to be complete for long. The spirit of piety kindly tolerates human frailty. The spirit of reverential fear of God eagerly consumes improvident ignorance and fully replaces it. Wisdom builds the house.[25] Understanding finds directions.[26] Counsel performs deeds discerned as good. Strength possesses its soul in patience.[27] By knowledge the riches of faith and salvation are acquired. Through piety prosperity of present and future life is established. By fear humility is preserved, and all sin driven away. Because *the beginning of wisdom is the fear of the Lord.*[28]

This is as far as the homily goes.

15. The list is numbered in the manuscripts.
16. Ps 7:14.
17. Ps 119:147.
18. Ps 51:6.
19. Ps 17:9.
20. Ps 31:12.
21. Ps 38:7.
22. Ps 25:7.
23. The seven gifts are now brought to bear on the seven states. This is done by supplying an appropriate adverb in each case to act as a bridge in order to facilitate the establishment of a connection.
24. V. Pet *Fab* no. 8 p. 7. The seven lamps in the tabernacle (Ex 25:37) provide an illustration of the role of the Holy Spirit with the seven gifts. There is nothing about north and south in the biblical text. Victorinus simply mentions the seven lamps.
25. Cf. Prov 14:1. The conclusion of the homily is another treatment of the seven gifts. Apart from the listing of the gifts, it is not connected with any of the preceding material.
26. Cf. Prov. 1:5.
27. Cf. Luke 21:19.
28. Cf. Ps 111:10.

BIBLIOGRAPHY

See the abbreviations in the front matter, pp. x–xiv.

Adomnan [Adomnanus]. *De Locis Sanctis libri 3*. Edited by L. Bieler. CCSL 175.
———. *Adomnan's Life of Columba*. Edited and translated by Alan Orr Ander-
son and Marjorie Ogilvie Anderson; revised by Marjorie Ogilvie Ander-
son. London: Nelson, 1991.
Aldhelmus. *Adhelmi Opera*. Edited by Rudolfus Ehwald. Monumenta Germaniae
Historica. Auctores Antiquissimi 15 [1919]. Munich: 1984.
Allen, Don Cameron. *The Legend of Noah. Renaissance Rationalism in Art, Sci-
ence and Letters*. Urbana: University of Illinois Press, 1963.
Alter, Robert. *The Art of Biblical Narrative*. New York: Basic Books, 1981.
Ambrose. *De patriarchis*. Edited by C. Schenkl. CSEL 32.
———. *De Spiritu Sancto*. Edited by O. Faller. CSEL 79.
Amos, T. L. "The Catechesis Cracoviensis and Hiberno-Latin Exegesis on the
Pater Noster," *PIBA* 13 (1990): pp. 77–107.
Arnobius Junior, *Expositiunculae in Evangelium Iohannis Evangelistae, Matthaei
et Lucae*. Edited by K.-D. Daur. CCSL 25 A.
Augustine. *Adnotationes in Iob*. Edited by I. Zycha. CSEL 28.
———. *Contra litteras Petiliani*. Edited by M. Petschenig. CSEL 52.
———. *De civitate Dei libri 22*. Edited by B. Dombart and A. Kalb. CCSL 47–
48.
———. *De consensu Evangelistarum*. Edited by F. Weihrich. CSEL 43.
———. *De diversis quaestionibus 83 liber*. Edited by A. Mutzenbecher. CCSL
44 A.

————. *Ennarrationes in Psalmos.* Edited by F. Dekkers and I. Fraipont. CCSL 38–40.

————. *In Iohannis Evangelium tractatus 124.* Edited by R. Willems. CCSL 38–40.

————. *Sermo de symbolo ad catechumenos.* Edited by R. Vander Plaetse. CCSL 46.

————. *Sermones.* PL 38:332–1484.

Bede, The Venerable. *Commentary on the Acts of the Apostles.* Translated, with an introduction and notes, by Lawrence T. Martin. Cistercian Studies Series 117. Kalamazoo, Mich.: Cistercian Publications, 1989. (See also Pseudo-Beda.)

Biblia Sacra. See Weber, Robertus.

Bieler, Ludwig, ed. *The Irish Penitentials* Dublin: Dublin Institute for Advanced Studies, [1963] 1975.

Bieler, Ludwig, and F. Kelly, eds. *The Patrician Texts in the Book of Armagh.* Dublin: Dublin Institute for Advanced Studies, 1979.

Bischoff, Bernhard. "Turning-Points in the History of Latin Exegesis in the Early Middle Ages." In Martin McNamara, ed. *Biblical Studies: The Medieval Irish Contribution.* PIBA 1. Dublin: Dominican Publications, 1976, pp. 73–160. [This is the English translation by Colm O'Grady of "Wendepunkte."

————. "Wendepunkte in der Geschichte der lateinischen Exegese im Frühmittelalter." *Sacris Erudiri* 6 (1954):189–279; rev., *Mittelalterliche Studien,* vol. 1. Stuttgart: Hiersemann, 1966, pp. 205–273.

Bischoff, Bernhard, and Michael Lapidge, eds. *Biblical Commentaries from the Canterbury School of Theodore and Hadrian.* Cambridge Studies in Anglo-Saxon England. Cambridge: Cambridge University Press, 1994.

Brearley, Denis. "The 'Expositio Iohannis' in Angers BM 275. A Commentary on the Gospel of St. John showing Irish influence," *Recherches Augustiniennes* 22 (1987):151–221.

Brooks, Roger, and John J. Collins, eds. *Hebrew Bible or Old Testament? Studying the Bible in Judaism and Christianity.* Notre Dame, Ind.: University of Notre Dame Press, 1990.

Caesarius of Arles, *Sermones.* Edited by G. Morin. CCSL 103–104.

Cahill, Michael. "The Identification of the First Markan Commentary," *Revue Biblique* 101, no. 2 (1994):258–68.

————. "The Identification of an Interpolated Homily in an Early Commentary on Mark." *Proceedings of the Conference on Patristic, Medieval and Renaissance Studies* 15. Villanova, Pa.: Villanova University, 1990.

————. "Is the First Commentary on Mark an Irish Work? Some New Considerations," *Peritia* 8 (1994):35–45.

————. "The Introductory Material to an Early (Irish) Commentary on Mark," *PIBA* 14 Dublin: Dominican Publicatons, 1991, pp. 93–114.

————. "Reader-Response Criticism and the Allegorizing Reader," *Theological Studies* 57, no. 1 (March 1996):89–96.

Catechesis Celtica. See Wilmart, A.

Catechesis Cracoviensis. See Amos, T. L.

Chapman, Dom John. *Notes on the Early History of the Vulgate Gospels*. Oxford: Clarendon, 1908.

Clark, Francis. *The Pseudo-Gregorian Dialogues*, vols. 1 and 2. Studies in the History of Christian Thought 37–38. Leiden: Brill, 1987.

Coccia, Edmondo. "La cultura irlandese precarolingia. Miracolo o mito?" *Studi Medievali* 3, no. 8 (1987):259–420. ("Il commentario al Vangelo de S. Marco," pp. 343–345.)

"Commentarius in Iohannem," *Scriptores Hiberniae Minores*. Edited by J. Kelly. CCSL 108C.

"Commentarius in Lucam," *Scriptores Hiberniae Minores*. Edited by J. Kelly. CCSL 108C.

Cross, James E. *Cambridge Pembroke College Ms. 25: A Carolingian Sermonary Used by Anglo-Saxon Preachers*. London: King's College, 1987.

———. "Research-Report on Cambridge Pembroke College ms 25," *Hiberno-Latin Newsletter* no. 1, (fall 1986):8–9.

Cyprian of Carthage. *De opere et eleemosynis*. Edited by M. Simonetti. CCSL 3 A.

Daniélou, Jean. *The Theology of Jewish Christianity*. London: D.L.T., 1964.

Dekkers, Eligius (and Aemilius Gaar). *Clavis Patrum Latinorum,* CCSL (3d ed., 1995).

Dewey, Joanna. "Recent Studies on Mark," *Religious Studies Review* 17, no. 1 (January 1991):12–16.

Eucherius. "Formulae," "Instructionum ad Salonium libri 2," and "De laude heremi." In *Sancti Eucherii Lugdunensis Opera Omnia*. Pars I. Edited by C. Wotke. CSEL 31.

Fischer, Bonifatius. *Verzeichnis der Sigel für Kirchenschriftsteller*, vol. 1. Part 1 of *Vetus Latina: Die Reste der altlateinischen Bibel*. Freiburg: Herder, 1963.

Gorman, Michael. "The Commentary on the Pentateuch Attributed to Bede in PL 91.189–394," *Revue Bénédictine* 106 nos. 1–2. (1996):61–108.

Grant, Mary, ed. and trans. *The Myths of Hyginus*. Humanistic Studies 34; Lawrence: University of Kansas Publications, 1960.

Grant, Robert, with David Tracy. *A Short History of the Interpretation of the Bible* (2d ed. rev.). Philadelphia: Fortress, 1984.

Gregorius Iliberritanus. *Tractatus Origenis*. Edited by V. Bulhart. CCSL 69.

Gregory the Great. *Expositio in Canticum Canticorum*. Edited by P. Verbraken. CCSL 144.

———. *Forty Gospel Homilies*. Translated from the Latin by Dom David Hurst. Cistercian Studies Series 123. Kalamazoo, Mich.: Cistercian Publications, 1990.

———. *Homiliae in Evangelia 40*. PL 76.

———. *Moralium libri sive Expositio in librum Iob*. Edited by M. Adriaen. CCSL 143A–B.

———. *Pastoral Care*. Translated and annotated by Henry Davis. Ancient Christian Writers 11. Westminster, Md.: Newman, 1950.

————. *Règle Pastorale*. Edited by B. Judic, F. Rommel, and C. Morel. SC 381 and 382.

————. *Sancti Gregorii Magni Homiliae in Hiezechielem Prophetam*. Edited by M. Adriaen. CCSL 142.

Grogan, Brian. "Eschatological Teaching in the Early Irish Church." In *Biblical Studies: The Medieval Irish Contribution*. Edited by Martin McNamara. *PIBA* 1. Dublin: Dominican Publications, 1976.

Herbert, Máire, and Martin McNamara. *Irish Biblical Apocrypha: Selected Texts in Translation*. Edinburgh: T. & T. Clark, 1989.

Hilaire de Poitiers. *Sur Matthieu*. Edited by J. Doignon. SC 254, 258.

Hillgarth, J. N., ed. "Modes of Evangelization of Western Europe in the Seventh Century." In Proinséas Ní Chatháin and Michael Richter, eds. *Irland und Christenheit: Bibelstudien und Mission ((Ireland and Christendom: The Bible and the Missions)*. Stuttgart: Klett-Cotta, 1987, pp. 311–331.

Horace. *Christopher Smart's Verse Translation of Horace's "Odes": Text and Introduction*. Edited by Arthur Sherbo. Victoria, Canada: English Literary Studies, University of Victoria, 1979.

Jerome. *Commentariorum in Hiezechielem libri 14*. Edited by F. Glorie. CCSL 75.

————. *Commentariorum in Matheum libri 4*. Edited by D. Hurst and M. Adriaen. CCSL 77.

————. *Commentariorum in Zachariam prophetam libri 3*. Edited by M. Adriaen. CCSL 76A.

————. *Epistulae*. Edited by I. Hilberg. CSEL 54–56.

————. *Liber Interpretationis Hebraicorum Nominum*. Edited by P. de Lagarde. CCSL 72.

————. *Tractatus in Marci Evangelium*. Edited by G. Morin. CCSL 78.

Josephus. *The Jewish War*. Translated by H. St. J. Thackeray. Loeb Classical Library 2–3, Cambridge: Harvard University Press, [1927] 1961.

Kealy, Seán P. *Mark's Gospel: A History of Its Interpretation. From the Beginning until 1979*. New York: Paulist Press, 1982.

Kelly, Joseph F. "Pelagius, Pelagianism and the Early Christian Irish." *Mediaevalia. A Journal of Medieval Studies* 4 (1978):99–124.

Labriola, Albert S., and John W. Smeltz, eds. *The Bible of the Poor (Biblia Pauperum): A Facsimile and Edition of the British Library Blockbook C.9.d.2. Translation and Commentary*. Pittsburgh: Duquesne University Press, 1990.

Lambert, Bernard. *Bibliotheca Hieronymiana Manuscripta. La tradition manuscrite des oeuvres de Saint Jérôme*. Vol. 3B (= *Instrumenta Patristica* IV). Steenbrugis: Martinus Níjhoff, 1970, pp. 376–381.

Lapidge, Michael, and Richard Sharpe. *A Bibliography of Celtic-Latin Literature 400–1200*. Dublin: Royal Irish Academy, 1985.

Leclercq, Jean. *The Love of Learning and the Desire for God*. New York: Mentor, 1961.

Le Goff, Jacques. *The Birth of Purgatory*. Chicago: University of Chicago Press, 1984.

Liber Quare. Edited by G. Götz. CCCM 60.

Liddel, Henry G., and Robert Scott. *A Greek-English Lexicon.* Oxford: Clarendon [1940] 1961.

Luz, Ulrich. *Matthew in History: Interpretation, Influence, and Effects.* Minneapolis: Fortress, 1994.

McNally, Robert E. "The Evangelists in the Hiberno-Latin Tradition." In *Festschrift Bernhard Bischoff.* Edited by J. Autenrieth and F. Brunhölzl. Stuttgart: Hiersemann, 1971.

McNamara, Martin. "Celtic Scriptures: Text and Commentaries." In James P. Mackey, ed., *An Introduction to Celtic Christianity.* Edinburgh: T. & T. Clark, 1989, pp. 414–440.

———. "The Inverted Eucharistic Formula 'Conversio Corporis Christi in Panem et Sanguinis in Vinum': The Exegetical and Liturgical Background in Irish Usage." In *Proceedings of the Royal Irish Academy 87 C, No. 10.* Dublin: Royal Irish Academy, 1987.

———. *Studies on Texts of Early Irish Latin Gospels (A.D. 600–1200).* Steenbrugis: Kluwer, 1990.

Morin, G. "Un commentaire romain sur S. Marc de la première moitié du Ve siècle." *Revue Bénédictine* 27 (1910):352–362.

———. "Un traité inédit d'Arnobe le Jeune. Le 'Libellus ad Gregoriam.'" *Revue Bénédictine* 27 (1910):153–171.

Mythographi Vaticani I and II. Edited by P. Kulcsár. CCSL 91 C.

O'Dwyer, Peter. *Célí Dé: Spiritual Reform in Ireland, 750–900,* 2d ed. Dublin: Editions Táiliúra, 1981.

Olsen, Glenn. "The Idea of the Ecclesia Primitiva in the Writings of Twelfth-Century Canonists." *Traditio* 25 (1969):61–86.

———. "Reference to the Ecclesia Primitiva in Eighth Century Irish Gospel Exegesis." *Thought* 54 (1979):303–312.

Origen. *Commentary on the Gospel according to John, Books 1–10.* Translated by Ronald E. Heine. The Fathers of the Church 80. Washington, D.C.: Catholic University of America, 1989.

———. *Homélies sur Josué.* Texte Latin. Edited by Annie Jaubert. SC 71.

———. *Homélies sur le Lévitique.* Texte Latin. Edited by M. Borret. SC 286–287.

———. *Homélies sur l'Exode.* Edited by H. de Lubac and P. Fortier. SC 321.

———. *Homilies on Genesis and Exodus.* Translated by Ronald E. Heine. The Fathers of the Church 71. Washington, D.C.: Catholic University of America, 1982.

———. *In Genesim.* PG 12.

———. *The Song of Songs: Commentary and Homilies.* Translated by R. P. Lawson. Ancient Christian Writers 26. Westminster, Md.: Newman, 1957.

Paschasius Radbertus. *Expositio in Matheo.* Edited by B. Paulus. CCCM 56, 56A, 56B.

Peter Chrysologus. *Selected Sermons.* Translated by George E. Ganss. The Fathers of the Church 17. Washington, D.C.: Catholic University of America, 1953.

Petrus Chrysologus. *Collectio Sermonum*. Edited by A. Olivar. CCSL 24, 24A, 24B.

Pseudo-Alcuinus. *De Septem Sigillis*. PL 101:1169–1170.

Pseudo-Beda. *Collectanea*. PL 94:539–576.

Pseudo-Hieronymus. *Expositio quatuor Euangeliorum*. PL 30:531–590.

Pseudo-Hilary of Arles. *Tractatus in septem epistolas canonicas*. Edited by R. McNally. CCSL 108 B.

Pseudo-Isidore. *Liber de ortu et obitu Patrum*. PL 83.

Pseudo-Jerome. See Pseudo-Hieronymus.

"Quaestiones vel glosae in evangelio nomine," "Praefacio secundum Marcum," and "In Evangelia Excerpta." In *Scriptores Hiberniae Minores*. Edited by R. McNally. CCSL 108 B.

Regul, Jürgen. *Die Antimarcionitischen Evangelienprologe. Vetus Latina. Aus dei Geschichte der lateinischen Bibel 6*. Freiburg: Herder, 1969.

Rittmueller, Jean, "The Gospel Commentary of Máel Brigte Ua Máeluanaig and Its Hiberno-Latin Background," *Peritia* 2 (1983):184–214.

Robbins, Vernon K. "Text and Context in Recent Studies of the Gospel of Mark." *Religious Studies Review* 17 no. 1 (January 1991):16–23.

Rupertus Tuitiensis. *Liber de divinis officiis*. Edited by H. Haacke. CCCM 7.

Sedulius. "Paschalis Carminis Libri Quinque cum Hymnis." In J. Huemer, ed. *Sedulii Opera Omnia*. CSEL 10. New York: Johnson Reprint, [1885] 1967.

Stancliffe, Clare. "Early 'Irish' Exegesis." *Studia Patristica* 12:361–370 (= *Texte und Untersuchungen zur Geschichte der alterchristlichen Literatur*, Band 115. Berlin: Akademie Verlag, 1975, pp. 361–370.

Stokes, Whitely, and John Strachan, eds. *Thesaurus Palaeohibernicus: A Collection of Old-Irish Glosses. Scholia Prose and Verse*. Vol. 1 of *Biblical Glosses and Scholia* Dublin: Institute for Advanced Studies, 1975.

Victorinus. *Victorini Episcopi Petauionsis Opera*. Edited by J. Hausleiter. CSEL 49.

Walsh, Maura, and Dáibhí Ó Cróinín, eds. *Cummian's Letter "De Controversia Paschali" and the "De Ratione Conputandi."* Studies and Texts 86. Toronto: Pontifical Institute of Medieval Studies, 1988.

Warner, George F. ed. *The Stowe Missal: Ms D.II.3 in the Library of the Royal Irish Academy, Dublin*. Wolfeboro, N.H.: The Henry Bradshaw Society and The Boydell Press, [1906] 1989.

Weber, Robertus, et al., eds. *Biblia Sacra iuxta Vulgatam Versionem, I–II*. Stuttgart: Deutsche Bibelgesellschaft, 1985.

Wilmart, André. "Catéchèses Celtiques" (Reg. Lat. 49). In *Analecta Reginensia. Extraits des manuscrits latins de la reine Christine conservés au Vatican*. Studi e Testi 59. Città del Vaticano: Biblioteca Apostolica Vaticana, 1933, pp. 29–112.

Wohlenberg, G. "Ein vergessener lateinischer Markuskommentar." *Neue Kirchliche Zeitschrift* 18 (1907):427–469.

Wordsworth, J., and H. White. *Novum Testamentum Domini Nostri Iesu Christi latine*. Pars Prior. Oxford: Clarendon, 1928.

Wright, Charles D. "Hiberno-Latin and Irish-Influenced Biblical Commentaries, Florilegia, and Homily Collections." In Frederick M. Biggs et al., eds. *Sources of Anglo-Saxon Culture: A Trial Version.* Medieval and Renaissance Texts and Studies 74. Binghamton: State University of New York, 1990.
——. *The Irish Tradition in Old English Literature.* Cambridge Studies in Anglo-Saxon England 6. Cambridge: Cambridge University Press, 1993.

INDEX OF
BIBLICAL TEXTS

Excludes Appendix

SELECT INDEX TO ANNOTATIONS

Excludes Appendix